# BUILDING A PROJECT WORK BREAKDOWN STRUCTURE

## VISUALIZING OBJECTIVES, DELIVERABLES, ACTIVITIES, AND SCHEDULES

# ESI International Project Management Series

Series Editor
J. LeRoy Ward, Executive Vice President
ESI International
Arlington, Virginia

**Practical Guide to Project Planning**
Ricardo Viana Vargas
1-4200-4504-0

**The Complete Project Management Office Handbook, Second Edition**
Gerard M. Hill
1-4200-4680-2

**Determining Project Requirements**
Hans Jonasson
1-4200-4502-4

**A Standard for Enterprise Project Management**
Michael S. Zambruski
1-4200-7245-5

**Building a Project Work Breakdown Structure: Visualizing Objectives, Deliverables, Activities, and Schedules**
Dennis P. Miller
1-4200-6969-3

## Other ESI International Titles Available from
## Auerbach Publications, Taylor & Francis Group

**PMP® Challenge! Fourth Edition**
J. LeRoy Ward and Ginger Levin
ISBN: 1-8903-6740-0

**PMP® Exam: Practice Test and Study Guide, Seventh Edition**
J. LeRoy Ward
ISBN: 1-8903-6741-9

**The Project Management Drill Book: A Self-Study Guide**
Carl L. Pritchard
ISBN: 1-8903-6734-6

**Project Management Terms: A Working Glossary, Second Edition**
J. LeRoy Ward
ISBN: 1-8903-6725-7

**Project Management Tools CD, Version 4.3**
ESI International
ISBN: 1-8903-6736-2

**Risk Management: Concepts and Guidance, Third Edition**
Carl L. Pritchard
ISBN: 1-8903-0700 7

# BUILDING A PROJECT WORK BREAKDOWN STRUCTURE
## VISUALIZING OBJECTIVES, DELIVERABLES, ACTIVITIES, AND SCHEDULES

**DENNIS P. MILLER**

CRC Press
Taylor & Francis Group
Boca Raton   London   New York

CRC Press is an imprint of the
Taylor & Francis Group, an **informa** business

AN AUERBACH BOOK

Auerbach Publications
Taylor & Francis Group
6000 Broken Sound Parkway NW, Suite 300
Boca Raton, FL 33487-2742

© 2009 by Taylor & Francis Group, LLC
Auerbach is an imprint of Taylor & Francis Group, an Informa business

---

**Library of Congress Cataloging-in-Publication Data**

---

Miller, Dennis P.
    Building a project work breakdown structure : visualizing objectives,
    deliverables, activities, and schedules / Dennis P. Miller.
       p. cm. -- (ESI international project management series ; 5)
    Includes bibliographical references and index.
    ISBN 978-1-4200-6969-3 (hbk. : alk. paper) 1. Project management. 2. Work
    breakdown structure. I. Title.

    HD69.P75M536 2008
    658.4'04--dc22
                                     2008014116

---

Visit the Taylor & Francis Web site at
http://www.taylorandfrancis.com

and the Auerbach Web site at
http://www.auerbach-publications.com

# Dedication

To my wife, Sharon.
Her support has always been the main drive in my life.

**Dennis Miller**

# Contents

## SECTION I: PREPLANNING ACTIVITIES AND ISSUES

## SECTION II: EXECUTING THE EIGHT STEP PROCESS

## SECTION III: POST-PLANNING ACTIVITIES

# SECTION IV: SOME BASIC PROJECT MANAGEMENT ISSUES

# List of Figures

# Preface: Why, How, and What I Developed

## Why I Developed

I think I have evolved the process (described in this book) because I personally do not understand a concept until I can see some representative image of it. I also noticed that I am not alone — most individuals find it difficult to understand ideas, concepts, and even actual activities until these elements are physically (visually) represented. This visual representation can become an end in itself. For example, if you want to sell your home, your realtor will tell you to leave your furniture in place. This allows potential buyers to consider their own furniture against yours and make the necessary mental adjustments, whereas an entirely bare room leaves little reference for size, color, and fit. Few people have the gift of visualizing physical objects from text and most of us need a helping technique. Moving from the general to the specific, I particularly noticed that teams in industrial settings need a unifying goal for them to pull together as a team. Although individuals are cooperative on the sports field, on the job, they seldom display the same teamwork. I really do not know what causes this different response in teams. Maybe it is as simple as job pressure, or competition, or the fear of losing a paycheck. As I became a project manager, I felt an immediate need for a technique that would motivate my teams toward a common goal. I needed a technique that would lead to the end result, yet would be engaging and somewhat entertaining.

## How I Developed

I developed the process (subsequently called the Eight Step Process) over a period of 20 years — while executing my own projects and helping other project managers plan their projects. I refined it by facilitating the planning of well over a hundred projects. These projects ranged from software development to social events.

This chance to plan many, varied projects expanded my project planning experience many times over what I would have realized as a project manager planning my own projects.

## What I Developed

The Eight Step Process utilizes a simple office supply product called the Post-It® (a 3M trademarked product) — immediately I recognized it as a planning tool. My approach to its use is different — this planning process combines processes, methods, and techniques all together into an initiative series of steps. When I first started using Post-Its, I did what most project managers instinctively do: pass out packages of Post-Its to the team members and instruct them to "Turn each Post-It into an activity." My results were the same as theirs — loads of Post-Its with little to no order. Only after many hours and sometimes days of sorting was I ready to show the plan to the project team. Meanwhile, the project itself may have changed and maybe even the team members had changed. Whose project plan was it now? Certainly not that of the original project planners! Because of the long delay between the planning session and the realization of the plan, no one would buy in to the final plan. The original planners would neither recognize nor feel any commitment to the plan. I had to learn how to shorten the delay between the planning session and the start of the project. In this regard, timing was everything. I had to develop a process that would produce an initial plan *during* the planning session.

## Why an Eight Step Process?

This Eight Step Process starts with a concentrated effort to define the project through its deliverables. Its final step validates the project's initial target date by critical path analysis (CPA). The middle steps "walk" the project team through a process of activity definition, resource allocation, and activity orientation (a network). The results either can be the input data for project management software or manually generated visuals of the project's objectives, deliverables, activities, and schedule. This process was developed during repeated engagements as either the project manager for the project (under planning) or as the planning session facilitator (as a consultant). Its application in more than a hundred planning sessions has provided satisfactory initial project plans. It truly is a highly stylized process and open for further development — by you. If you do not yet have your own planning process, take from the Eight Step Process those steps that will work for you. Then write a book of your own and share your process with other practicing project managers.

# Why Visual (versus Textual)?

Most people would agree that the presentation of vital information is best received, understood, remembered, and utilized when delivered in a visual (versus a textual) format. Some researchers declare that 85 to 90 percent of the people in developed countries are 100-percent visual. This does not mean they cannot read, only that they have developed (or have been taught) to live in a visual mode. If this is so, then why not use techniques in your project management (planning, communicating, etc.) that best match this reality? Think of yourself: are you visual or textual? How about your client (clients) — are they visual or textual? Sadly, there is no recognized test for visual versus textual. However, you can perform your own unscientific test. Think back to your last presentation to your client. How did they respond to your visuals? Did they ask for text to explain your visuals? Did they seem satisfied by your visual presentation? When presented only with textual information, did they either seem unsatisfied or specifically ask "for more visual representation"? Answers to any of these questions naturally will lead you to understand their particular orientation — visual versus textual.

# The Tone and Syntax of the Book

My objective in writing this book is to pass on to the reader a technique I have found valuable. I only can hope that through the diligent application of the Eight Step Process, you will learn immediately usable skills. These skills should help you realize tangible benefits for your next project. My intention for the tone of the book is one that is open and instructional in nature, and my hope is that you find this true as you proceed through it.

The use of first- and second-person subject, object, and possessive personal pronouns (for example, I, me, mine, etc.) is considered "bad form" in a book of this kind. My way of getting around this difficulty is to give you a "code phrase." The code phrase will be "experience tells us." When you see "experience tells us," you will know that I am referring to some experience of mine.

Please excuse my syntax; I am a project manager trying now to become a writer. I will probably violate every writing rule on the books but I hope it will not be too painful for you. I believe there are "doers" and there are "writers." Some doers never write and that is a shame. Some writers never do and for them to write is a shame. I am a doer who is trying his best to write — thank you for your patience.

# Acknowledgments

I would like to acknowledge the illustrations that our daughter, Peri, prepared for this book. Her approach to her life, her art, and her family has been a delightful realization for her life. Thank you for being our daughter, Peri Denise Miller!

Acknowledgments

# About the Author

**Dennis Miller** is a Certified Project Manager (PMP), an experienced project manager, an author, a lecturer, and an educator. IBM certified Miller as one of its few certified project managers (#34). The PMI (Project Management Institute) certified (PMP #437) him in 1990.

Miller's career at IBM was in manufacturing, information technology, PC product development, education, consulting, and program management. He "graduated" from IBM in 1996 as a Senior Technical Professional.

Miller joined the consulting firm of Cap Gemini as a director. While at Cap Gemini, he led Y2K, system integration, and methodology improvement projects. As a Cap Gemini director, client relationship management and sales efforts were his major work effort.

In 1999, Miller started his own consulting firm. He specializes in project management training and project start-up engagements. As a consultant for IBM, Cap Gemini, and himself, he has led more than a hundred project start-up engagements.

Miller graduated from Wichita State University with a B.S. in Chemistry and from Syracuse University with an M.S. in Engineering Administration.

Dennis and his wife Sharon live in Pinehurst, North Carolina. When not traveling to work, he plays golf and tennis. His hobbies include woodworking, travel, and writing.

Miller's first book, *Visual Project Planning & Scheduling*, was published by his spouse (The 15th Street Press) and it was the basis for project management classes at both IBM and Cap Gemini.

# Opening

## Some Background on the Work Breakdown Structure (WBS)

The origin and exact date of development of the WBS (Work Breakdown Structure) are not exactly clear. It appears that it was developed in response to some unstated problem within the United States Department of Defense (DoD). Most authors (writing on this subject) and their articles do not address the source of the WBS. It was not until 2002 that a booklet* clarified what had been, until that time, simply "folklore." Haugan's booklet clarified a number of misconceptions that had developed during the previous 45 years. This booklet is an excellent reference for exact details. However, we now know that the WBS was developed as a component of a larger effort to control DoD projects from the early 1960s through to today. The official reference (as of 2002) was the DoD's site for the WBS. The exact World Wide Web reference has changed and, at this writing, is lost. A recent search for "Work Breakdown Structure" on the World Wide Web (WWW) produced more than 2,260,000 sites. This is an expression of both the commercialism of the WWW and the popularity of the WBS.

My first knowledge of the WBS was when an associate described FTP (File Transfer Protocol) site — an early form of the Internet. He described a diagram (Figure O.1) displaying the WBS as composed of three distinct components: (1) the Product Breakdown Structure (PBS), (2) the Activity Breakdown Structure (ABS), and (3) the Organizational Breakdown Structure (OBS).

This original diagram (Figure O.1) made clear the relationship between the deliverables (PBS) and the activities (ABS) that produce the deliverables. However, it did not make clear what the OBS was and how it related to the other two components. Later interpretations of the WBS seemed to make the tie-in among all three components. Most articles, books, and even most of the many U.S. Government

---

* Haugan, Gregory T. *Effective Work Breakdown Structures,* Vienna, VA: Management Concepts, 2002.

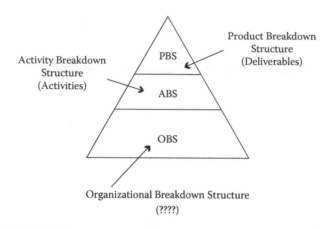

**Figure O.1  Earliest version of the WBS.**

WWW sites express the OBS as the organization (people) performing the activities that produce the deliverables. These same WWW sites show the same sample OBS diagram originally displayed in the earliest WBS publications — the identical OBS diagram!

## *Misinterpretations Developed over Time*

Probably because of the secret nature of its early development and the resulting lack of clear information (now 45 years later), there have been a number of misinterpretations of the original intent and definition of the WBS.

The first misinterpretation concerns "the use of the OBS." The DoD Web site of 2002 clarified the use of the OBS. It also made it clear that the WBS was not developed as a tool for project planning, but instead a tool for project control. It further stated that the OBS is an accounting tool — a tool whereby accountants can understand the relationship between the deliverables (what they are paying for) and the account. The accounts in this matter are appropriations from the U.S. Congress. This clarification of the use of the OBS probably helps us understand the problem they were trying to solve. During that time, the U.S. Government was involved in very large-scale defense expenditures. One can only project the confusion the accountants (Government Accountability Office) for the U.S. Congress were feeling without some sort of reference to the money they were authorizing.

The second misinterpretation was that "the WBS is oriented around activities." One cannot see precisely in the published literature where this idea began. There are two possibilities: (1) the first published documents displayed a component called the Activity Breakdown Structure, and (2) the development of personal computer (PC)–based project management software. The first possibility is a far reach in terms of how it could contribute to this misinterpretation. The second possibility (PC project management software) is much easier to understand. PC-based project management software is itself organized around "doing something." This "doing something" translates into "activities." A company called ABT™ (since sold and renamed) developed one of the first commercial PC-based programs in the United Kingdom. ABT operator manuals described only activities and did not mention deliverables. This interpretation of the WBS as activity oriented was furthered by VisiCorp™ (a U.S. developer) in its product (VisiSchedule™). There is good evidence that Microsoft™ adopted an activity orientation in its product (MS Project™). This was a time when operator manuals were printed on paper and you can see that in most cases, they used the exact same word to describe the WBS in activities (only) terms. This misinterpretation has been corrected — the Project Management Institute (PMI™) has published a practices manual and the DoD Web site further clarified the intent of the WBS as "deliverable oriented." The PMI has waffled somewhat on this issue by stating that the WBS can contain activities. On the other hand, the DoD Web site clearly states that the WBS does not contain activities.

The third misinterpretation is that "the bottommost level of the WBS is where all the work is defined." Some authors have argued that the term "work" has a different meaning when used with the WBS. Their definition is "something upon which labor is expended." This alternative definition of "work" would make it an object, a physical deliverable. This interpretation is in every project management book and test. It is an interpretation "locked in literature," never to be reversed (in my lifetime). Experience tells us that this interpretation is not correct … but wait and you will see.

## *Current Accepted Practice*

The current accepted practice as proclaimed in the PMI's practice standard document is that the WBS is deliverable oriented but can contain activities. However, when viewing that document's examples, you soon recognize that the examples are strictly activity based. If fifty leading, PM practitioners developed the document and PMI called it a "global standard," then one might well accept it as the current accepted practice for the WBS.

The earliest documents did not make clear the intent of the WBS; and in fact, it is difficult to discern the WBS from the other DoD processes. The latest DoD Web site makes a distinction between managing a project and controlling it. It goes further to say that the WBS is intended to control the project — control the cost aspects. It considers the WBS a cost accounting tool. An accountant would call the OBS, a component of the WBS, the "chart-of-accounts." The DoD extends the original intent by intimating that it is their tool and it was never intended as a project-planning tool, let alone a "practice standard." Ignoring this dissection of history and the question of its original intent, one soon realizes by actual practice

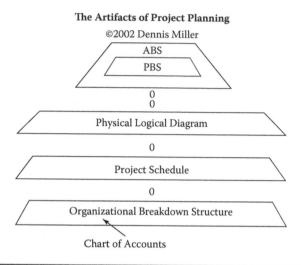

**Figure O.2   The artifacts of project planning (© Dennis Miller, 2002.)**

that the WBS has developed into our profession's number-one soft tool for planning a project.

## New View of How the WBS Fits in with a Practical Project Management Approach

You can either struggle with a standard practice in relationship to your own practice or develop a view that incorporates the acceptable practice and make it richer in terms of a practical project management approach. This author first presented the diagram in Figure O.2 in 2002 at PMI regional meetings, training sessions, and consulting engagements; it was readily accepted as a clear view of a project planning process in terms of its physical attributes.

You can see the orientation of the top two components of the WBS (i.e., PBS and ABS) are overlaid — the ABS over the PBS. This displays a reality: the ABS is always larger (more activities) than the PBS (deliverables). First, the PBS is developed to provide a well-founded representation of the project's deliverables. The deliverables are the bases for the activities. In this practical approach, they (PBS and ABS) are the foundation for the physical logical diagram (network). In fact, the activities form the physical logical diagram (subsequently called the Network).

The Network is complete with resources and activity durations. If PM software (MS Project™) is used, it can establish the project schedule and automatically provide the OBS (chart-of-accounts).

Figure O.3 is an overall view of the process on which this book is based — the Eight Step Process.

# Organization of the Book

This book is organized as follows.

## *Part One: Preplanning Activities and Issues*

Part One asks some important questions regarding your readiness for the planning session and some tough questions about your organization and its readiness to accept your planning results. Then it lays out what specific steps you need regarding communications, timing, planning facilities, and the planning documents you will need. It also presents the possible sources for the definition of the project's deliverables and the issue of remote planning situations (virtual teams). Its tone is one of caution. The intent is not to discourage you, but rather to prepare you for the tasks needed before conducting the planning session.

## *Part Two: Executing the Eight Step Process*

Part Two takes the reader through an eight-step process and it variations. It is the largest part of the book and the detail is extensive. In this part, each chapter discusses one step of the Eight Step Process. Each step is divided into the following sections:

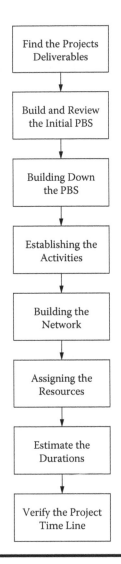

**Figure O.3   The Eight Step Process.**

- ■ Background
- ■ Just-it-time (JIT) training
- ■ Practice (the case study)
- ■ Specific facilitation instructions
- ■ Hints

Part Two is your manual for facilitating a project planning process (the Eight Step Process). This detailed set of instructions is a compilation of more than 20 years of experience in planning projects and conducting consulting engagements (project start-ups). This experience is condensed in the Eight Step Process and shared as specific problems and solutions related to each step.

## Organization of Each of the Eight Steps

- *Background.* The background explains the step in terms of what is it, why in this order, and its overall importance. Specific items in the background support other items in both the JIT and the facilitation instructions. This approach prepares the project manager for the inevitable questions.
- *Just-in-time (JIT) training.* There is considerable training needed to facilitate a planning session. Most of this very specific training does not exist in any publication. Just-in-time training was selected because of just what the title says — just in time. Training is the most valuable (immediately usable and remembered) if provided just when needed. Some of the training is simple but worthy of repeating. Some of the training is in the social sciences that project managers deploy — communications, understanding people, negotiating, problem solving, politics, etc.
- *Practice.* The practice section takes the reader through an eight-step project planning session. The intent of this section is to tie the instructional set to a real-life situation, help the reader "see through the eyes" of a project manager, and provide a better understanding of the project planning style represented by the Eight Step Process.
- *Specific facilitation instructions.* For this book to be of value as a facilitation manual, it is necessary to provide specific facilitation instructions. These instructions take the form of spoken instructions (to the team) and instructional diagrams. The combination of the two will provide the necessary JIT training to the project planning team through the "voice" of the project manager (facilitator). It is not necessary to deliver the instructions verbatim, but rather paraphrased and delivered by the project manager. The specific facilitation instructions are a "script" — intended for delivery the first few times by the project manager.
- *Hints.* The "hints" section is just that — hints. Hints are miscellaneous bits and pieces of problems and solutions you might encounter during the step. Not all hints are fully supported in previous sections. Some hints are really born of personal and shared experiences. This type of learning is not generally organized in any manner — it is experiential based.

## Part Three: Post-Planning Activities

The post-planning activities part reviews a set of follow-up items that logically follow the planning session. Again, there will be problems and solutions, difficult questions to ask and answer, and specific steps that need to happen soon after the planning session. Again, the tone here is caution. What the project manager does after the planning session is as important as all the preplanning and the session itself. Decisions made during the post-planning timeframe will help avoid serious problems during project implementation.

## Part Four: Some Basic Project Management Issues

This part brings forth questions regarding the Eight Step Process and project management. These frequently asked questions are normally directed to the project manager by the project planning team. Some questions are ones posed by other project managers who have used The Eight Step Process. Some questions could have been asked during Part Two or Part Three but are better handled here. Some questions seem simple on the surface but have an undertone of greater meaning — requiring some forethought and preplanning for the next planning session. The questions are phrased as Frequently Asked Questions (FAQs). The answers come from many years and many "times at bat."

# PREPLANNING ACTIVITIES AND ISSUES

I

# Chapter 1

# Preplanning Issues

## Opening Issues

There are a number of preplanning issues that should be addressed in any planning situation and are best discussed now (up front) in this book as you would discuss them up front in your project. Some of these issues will need addressing at the beginning of each project. Some issues need addressing now — as you are deciding whether to proceed with the recommendations of this book. These latter issues can be tough to answer on your part but you need to reach deep down inside yourself and honestly answer the questions implied by the issues. This honest discussion with yourself will tell you whether to adopt this process.

### Issue: Do Not Ask if You Do Not Plan to Use!

There is an old saying among personnel managers that "if you aren't going to act on a person's opinion, then don't ask their opinion." This also holds true for project planning: if you do not want to know (and use) just how your team would execute the project, then do not ask them to define a project plan. It is "deadly" for the team's spirit to conduct a team-based planning session like that promoted here and afterward discard the resulting plan. By "deadly," I mean, to ask and not use will destroy any possibility for project team buy-in. Buy-in is perhaps the strongest psychological "tool" a project manager can have, and it should be treated very carefully — it is a limited commodity that one spends carefully. There will be a lot more on buy-in later. This issue of asking for a team-based project plan brings into play the issue of your personal management style regarding planning.

## Issue: *Your Personal Management Style*

There are really two basic management styles regarding project planning. The first is *directive*. In this style, the project manager develops the project plan and essentially "presents it to the project team." The project manager expects team members to execute the plan and perform their assigned duties without dissent. This management style works fine for projects or tasks requiring no intelligent input on the part of the "worker." The directive style is an old management form and frankly not popular with today's intellectual workers.

The second style is *participatory*. The participatory style requires the project manager to engage with the project team and facilitate the project team members in *their* building of the project plan. This requires the project manager to delegate authority to the project team. This does not mean that the project manager must abdicate his or her base responsibility for the project — project managers can never delegate responsibility. It means that they recognize their project team as the true source of all the work. It means they respect and trust their team members to build a valid project plan that *they* will implement.

This book promotes the participatory style for project planning. If this is now your style, then continue reading — full speed ahead. If this style is contrary for you, then please continue reading with an open mind and a strong commitment to consider a much different style.

## Issue: *How Important Is the Project to Your Organization?*

This issue forces questions and answers for each project. Just how important is this project to your organization? Will a project failure damage the organization? How much project visibility does the organization possess? Who will be "damaged" by a project failure? Are the project's objectives aligned with the organization's goals — supporting a portion of those goals? Your answers to these questions will force you to modify your own approach to the process and specific methods proposed here.

## Issue: *Write Your Management Style into Your Project Charter*

The issues of style and project importance naturally lead to the issue of your "charter." Regarding projects, the term "charter" can have several meanings. The first meaning is simply the *implied power* that you wield as the project manager. In this form, it also can mean your objectives. The second meaning is as a formal document defining specifically your authority (and accountability). The charter, as a defining document, has only recently become a major component of the project manager's toolbox. There have been other names used for this document, such as terms-of-reference, rules-of-engagement, etc.

The charter and these issues are related by the degree of authority the project manager has to conduct a team-based project planning session. A successful project planning session, as proposed in this book, could require traveling (fly, drive, etc.) your team to a central location — today's project teams often are scattered over a large geographic area (e.g., the world). The matter of travel and its associated costs often is wrongly consigned to the general category of "project assumptions." The charter can open up this issue and then provide early decisions concerning traveling your project team. The decision can be "forced" by the inclusion of a statement of authority: "The project manager has the authority to travel the project team to a central location several times during the project." To complete the delegation of authority, the charter also should define the limits of each authority as a statement of accountability: "The project manager will budget the team's travel, manage it, and report quarterly actual-to-plan expenditures."

## Issue: Will Your Organization Accept Results?

Another issue now comes forward for resolution: will your organization (your management) accept your results? In most cases, an assigned project will come with a target end-date and a target cost; this is quite normal. There can be many reasons why this is so. It could be simply that there is no more money, and the date could be either when it is needed or when your manager committed it (for you). You probably can assume there is little real understanding about the content of the project and the resulting targets — they are simply targets. This frequently becomes an issue when you present different-than-expected results from your project planning session (end-date and cost).

This issue comes down to how much tolerance your organization has for variances to the original targets. If possible, understand immediately the source or reasoning behind the targets. Is there a business case for the project? If so, get a copy; it represents your organization's expectations for the project. Again, the project charter (now a document) can aid you in this matter. It could include a delegation of authority (statement of expected end-date and target cost) and an accountability statement (the allowable variations). In this manner, you will "surface" the issue of how receptive your organization will be to your planning results. Most often, the organization avoids this issue until the very end of the project. If you either sense or have knowledge that this will be a difficulty, you need to get out in front of it early — be proactive. Your project charter is a great way to be proactive about problems you have experienced in the past.

## *Issue: Can You Pull This Off?*

After considering these issues against your personality, your style, your charter, and your organization, you still have one more issue (at least) to clear: can you pull this off? The following chapters pose additional considerations. These issues are presented not as blocking actions, but only so that you can decide whether you can pull this off.

# Chapter 2

# Sources of Deliverables

## Project Deliverables

There can be many sources for the definition of your project deliverables. The reason for focusing on deliverables is that they are the foundation of the Eight Step Process. A more important reason is that the client is only interested in what the project will deliver — that is, the deliverables. These combined reasons drive this first step: find the project's deliverables.

A desirable but unrealistic expectation would be a complete list of the project deliverables. Therefore, we begin with what you might have available. The very best source of deliverables is a requirements document. A requirements document usually is written from the point of view of the client; it is what the client wants to happen. Ideally, it starts with a high-level statement of the objective, purpose, or goal — a tightly written document of major expectations.

### Requirements Document

A set of three to five project objectives would be an excellent starting point. A well-organized requirements generation process would begin with project objectives; move through wants, desires, and "must-have" requirements; and finally result in a condensed set of prioritized, agreed-to requirements. Experience tells us that a well-written requirements document is a rare thing. The requirements document is so important in some professions (e.g., Information Technology) that its generation is separate from the overall project — a separate project of its own. In this approach, the implementation portion of the overall project will not begin until the requirements (document) are completed and signed. In Information Technology, this would be a "perfect world, infrequently achieved."

### Client's Own Words

Lacking a requirements document, the next best source is your client's own words. In this case, you may be working with e-mails, letters, and documented client interviews. If that is all you have to work with, it will have to do. The problems with miscellaneous documents are that they are not organized, there may be a large number of documents, a great deal of the material is not related to the project, and there is no indication of priorities. All this means that you might have to sort through a mountain of material to get a little information. Again, lacking anything else, it will have to do.

### Objective Statement Only

Sometimes (and it seems all too often), you will have nothing more than a brief, high-level statement of objectives. In this case, you will have to depend on your own ideas and experience. If your work environment supports subject matter experts (SMEs), then you can draw them into the development of deliverables. Experience tells us that SMEs tend to orient themselves around activities. This can be difficult as you are now moving toward an orientation of deliverables *first*. Careful listening still will provide deliverables "out of their activities" — the deliverables are in their activities descriptions (verb-noun).

## Your Planning Team

Your last source of deliverables is your project planning team. This requires that you start the Eight Step Process (subsequently called "the Process") with your team at Step 1. Step 4 is a better starting point for your team! Starting at Step 1 will slow the planning session considerably, but lacking all of the above sources, you will have no choice. Using your project planning team members to develop your deliverables is not all bad if they have experience with the Process. Their experience will have taught them the concepts needed to get quickly past Step 1. On the other hand, there will be an advantage. One of the objectives of Step 4 is to generate team buy-in; and if the team develops the deliverables, then you have their *de facto* buy-in.

### No Definition at All

There is always the possibility that no deliverables are forthcoming from any of the above four sources. You then have to question: "Do I really have a project?" If the answer is still "yes" and you still want to proceed, do not try to proceed with a full project planning session. Experience tells us this could lead to a disaster that may not be recoverable. An alternate course would be to create a different project than originally assigned. The new first project becomes the generation of the requirements (deliverables). The second project is the implementation of the deliverables. Some of the best consultant firms do just this. Your client probably will complain immediately that the approach of two projects will increase the overall time. Experience tells us two things: (1) to proceed without a good set of deliverables will cause delays during the entire project, and (2) the combination of the two projects (definition of deliverables and implementation) will not take any longer to complete (fewer false starts and less rework) than the original project endpoint.

*Chapter 3*

# Timing of Planning Session

## A Question of Timing

The question is: how soon before the project start date should you conduct the planning session? A good answer is: as close to the start date as possible. Ideally, you should finish the planning session and start the project the next day. This would be ideal and surely not a "rule." The reason for completing the planning session so close to the project start date is simply that things change. The project definition (deliverables) can change. The available team members can change. The technology can change. Anything can change. The closer (planning session) to the start date, the less likely it is that major changes will occur. It is deadly to a project to plan the project, shelve the project plan, and then drag it out two or three months later for a project start. This would probably necessitate another planning session with probably the same team members — a team will have just so much patience. Try to conduct your planning session with no more than ten days' delay from the session end to the start of the project. Experience tells us that the most powerful statement ever heard uttered at the end of a planning session was, "Team, tomorrow we will start our project using the project plan you just finished developing."

## How Many Days?

One of your major preplanning decisions will be to determine how many days the planning session should take. Table 3.1 sets some guidelines for this decision.

Experience tells us that the major deciding factor in a project of any size is first the number of members on the team that need to be involved in the planning session. A one-day session is sufficient for a project of two weeks to three months'

**Table 3.1  Guidelines for Determining Duration of Planning Session**

| Number of Days for Session(s) | 1 Day | 2 Days | 3 Days | Many, 3-day sessions |
|---|---|---|---|---|
| Size of planning team | Less than 5 people | 5–10 but less than 20 people | 20–35 but less than 40 people | Greater than 40 people |
| Length of project | 2 weeks–3 months | 3–12 months | 7–12 months | 12–18 months |

duration and with less than five people. However, you will probably require a two-day session as your team size increases (up to 20). The increase in the length of the project is of course another deciding factor but still the number of people involved has the largest effect. If the team can be segmented (divided into two parts), then you can conduct two, one-day sessions. Today, many project teams are widely separated and this approach can work in that situation. If you choose this approach, it will take a careful combination of the separate team plans and you will have to provide that effort. The time necessary for the combining step will further delay the publication of the project plan and will lessen the chance for a complete team buy-in in a timely manner. You can apply this same approach to the three-day session. The same difficulties are in effect for combining and buy-in, but larger.

When you have very large project teams and you want them all involved, you may need many three-day sessions. Experience tells us that such project planning efforts can extend into months to develop just the project plan. Experience also tells that such large projects are either not successful (on time, within cost, or with a full set of deliverables) or never get started at all. You will notice that Table 3.1 does not go beyond three days. Experience tells us that a three-day session is just about all a project team can tolerate and a project manager can handle.

## How Many Hours per Day?

Another issue: should you plan on eight hours per day? Ideally, you could use all eight hours in a normal working day; but in reality, you should probably plan for only about six to six-and-a-half hours per day. The main reason for an abbreviated day is that the sessions are intense. This intensity causes fatigue for everyone involved, and you will find that six-and-a-half hours is very much the limit of their productivity and tolerance. In addition, participants are frequently trying also to maintain their normal work schedule — they are busy people. Experience tells us that starting at 9:00 a.m. and continuing to about 4:00 p.m. is a good schedule. This leaves about an hour for lunch — for refreshments and the necessary telephone calls and a few hours at the end of the day for other business. If perhaps you have traveled your team away from the home office, then you might consider another evening session of two to three hours.

# Chapter 4

## Specific Preparations

### Communications

As in all project management activities, good communication is essential. A planning session might be the first test of your communication style with this particular team. How you manage this vital communication event can determine how well your project gets started. You will need to understand the types of communications and what is the best type to deploy and when. Because you might be communicating with a large number of people and across a wide geographic area, a formal communication style is appropriate. The most formal style is a written request for their attendance. The timing of your planning session in relationship to the beginning of the project also will affect the timing and sense of urgency of your invitation. If you have only a few days before starting the planning session, then you might not have enough time for a formal, written invitation. In this case, you should call the individuals and follow up with a written invitation. If you have adequate time before the planning session, then a written invitation followed by a personal call might be best. There are as many variations as there are organizations. Your own personal communication style will guide you in this decision.

### Personal Calendars

Then the question becomes: how will the invitee respond? The question revolves, in part, around the invitee's personal calendar. People involved in projects are typically very busy; remember the old adage that "if you want something done, ask a busy person." This holds doubly true for project-oriented organizations. You will need to understand the dynamics of your organization (people). You need to understand the reality of their working situation — current availability, workload, and continuing commitments. The second important consideration is your need to understand the reality of their alignment to your project: can they participate in a continuous, meaningful manner? Do they understand the need that drives your project? Do they have personal (outside of work) commitments that ultimately will interfere with the project (timing)? In short, are they available, willing, and interested in your project? The concept of personal alignment is somewhat new to project management literature; but to the modern, intellectual worker, it can be their number-one consideration. Your success in getting on their personal calendar is critical. There will be many times when the very person you need cannot possibly attend your planning session — but there is an alternative. In this case, you need to "deploy" a subject matter expert (SME). An SME can substitute for the actual person in many situations — but this is only a "last resort." Step 4 discusses the issue of using an SME as a substitute.

## Planning Session Site

The location of the session site and its physical layout is important to a well-run planning session. The location is important in many ways. If you travel your project team, then the logistics of travel (cost, time, and distance from the normal working site) essentially can make the choice of site for you. Experience tells us that, with regard to the difficulty of travel, your concern for the participants is essential for team morale. Long distances, difficult locations (remote), and uncomfortable living situations will lead to poor morale. All these factors will cause you continuing difficulties during your planning session — and the last thing you want to handle is poor morale. A well-thought-out session plan should consider all these factors and, if possible, all such difficulties should be discussed in advance (with participants). The authority to travel a project team should be resolved up front in the project (i.e., in the project charter).

Now consider the physical aspects of the planning site. Even a comfortable, convenient planning site may not have the physical attributes required. Experience tells us that the main attribute is the size of the planning area (typically a room). Normal facilities would include a sufficient number of tables and chairs. Special equipment might include flipchart easels, projectors (slide, overhead, and maybe even liquid-crystal types). There must be enough room around the tables and chairs to allow for free movement of the team members. An especially difficult room contains equipment for teaching any type of personal computer (PC) class. PC rooms typically have permanent, fixed locations for the tables and very poor visibility of the classroom as a whole. An added difficulty is the close availability of PCs and the access they provide to the "outside world" — attention span is always a challenge during the planning session. More on the issue of attention span later.

The second most important attribute is whether there is sufficient "free wall space." Free wall space means that the walls are essentially clear and free of windows, pictures, photographs, and an excessive number of doors. Wall space is essential to the Eight Step Process; it is where we work. Experience tells us that very large planning teams require very large spaces to be comfortable and productive. The best is a large room with minimally occupied wall space — such as a handball court. Experience also tells us that a team of 55 people can plan a project with more than 1800 deliverables and more than 2800 activities in just four days in such a facility.

## Handouts

The question of providing handouts to the planning team is next. This preparation item highly depends on what documents are available. Some documents are "rich" in terms of relevant information and others will provide little necessary information. You will have to decide what document will be necessary to support the planning effort. Take care not to pass out a great volume of paper. The timing of the planning session is tight and there really is no time for a great deal of reading. If a definite need for extensive background reading exists, then provide an advance release of the materials. After deciding, ensure that *all* members receive a copy of *all* handouts. Experience reveals that it is important that all members receive the same materials. If you have a project charter, it should be included in the handouts.

## Supplies

How you conduct the planning session, where it will occur, and how many people are involved will affect the type and amount of supplies needed. Experience tells us that the following is a minimum set of supplies for the planning session itself:

- Post-Its® (3 × 3 inch): if the planning team is building the PBS, then provide one package per person.
- Post-Its (3 × 5 inch): provide one package (100) per person.
- Banner or flipchart paper: provide a full pad of flipchart paper or one roll of banner paper.
- Highlighter pens (medium point): provide one per person.
- Felt tip pens (fine point): provide one per person.
- Masking tape (1 inch): provide two or more rolls.
- Transparent tape (1 inch): provide two or three rolls.
- Writing pads and pencils: provide one set per person (optional).

The question as to what size Post-It to use depends on whether the planning team is going to build the product breakdown structure (PBS). If so, then you should use 3 × 3-inch Post-Its to represent the project's deliverables. Whether or not they build the PBS, you will need the 3 × 5-inch Post-Its. Experience tells us that 3M's Post-It™ notes are superior in quality to other copycats, and thus this book utilizes the "Post-It" term throughout (henceforth the trademark is implied). Either banner paper or flipchart paper is necessary to cover the walls and receive the Post-Its. Neither blackboards nor whiteboards are successful because both types of boards (no matter how clean) will retain some dust from the marker (chalk or dry marker). This dust will adhere to the sticky portion of the Post-It and immediately interfere with its sticking power. Another reason for the paper is that you will be drawing lines on the paper to show the logic of the activities one-to-another, and any drawing off the paper should be discouraged — for the obvious reasons. The highlighter pens are used to highlight portions of the documents (handouts) to help the team identify deliverables. The felt-tipped pens are used to write on the Post-Its. They should have fine points for clarity. Normal ballpoint pens will be sufficient but are not as visible as felt-tipped pens from a distance. Experience tells us Sharpie™ or Vis-à-vis™ are the preferred marking pens. The masking tape is used to mount the paper on the walls. Here again, you must be careful; some masking tape is strong enough to pull away the wallpaper, paint, and wallboard. Experience tells us that "painter's tape" is probably the strongest and easiest to remove, and will not destroy the wall surface. The transparent tape aids in retaining the Post-Its on the paper. Eventually, Post-Its will become "tired" (when moved too often) and fall off the paper. They will certainly fall off either after some time (a few days) or when the humidity rises. It is best to apply a small piece of transparent tape to the top of the Post-It after its position is "well established." The writing pads and pencils are optional but do "round out" any well-conducted session.

## Break Materials

The issue of providing break materials (snacks, drinks, and even lunch) depends on your style and the conditions of your session site. The first question is: should I provide either break materials or lunches? Your organization usually sets the "normal" policy regarding this matter. However, do not consider the session a normal situation (meeting). Experience tells us (especially when it is not the norm) that your planning team will quickly note and greatly appreciate any break materials. This simple matter can garner a great deal of goodwill. It also will demonstrate your authority and ability to go against the "norm." A strong arguing point for providing a simple lunch is that you will have a working lunch and the team can re-engage in the planning effort much sooner. The logistics of a full dinner are much more complicated. However, a dinner on the second day of a three-day session provides closure for the team.

A word on "closure" — closure in this instance is simply the time taken to provide recognition for a job well done. The person recognized will always remember the time you set aside for him or her to "take full measure of their contribution to the project with and from their peers." This is a matter of personal style — "a good add-on."

# EXECUTING THE EIGHT STEP PROCESS

# Chapter 5

## Step 1
## Find the Project's Deliverables

## Background
### Deliverable versus Activity Orientation

As described in the Opening, there has been considerable discussion about how a project plan should be oriented. Almost without exception, project management literature and PC software have promoted an orientation around activities. Only recently has there has been recognition that a better way to orient a project plan is by deliverables. "Orientation" means the bases or foundation for the project plan. Experience tells us that the client's interest in a project status presentation quickly wanes when presented by "all the work the project team must perform" — that is, the activities. Why would that occur? This is what the team is doing on their behalf. We are confused. Why is the client not intensely interested? The reason is that the clients are only interested in what the project brings to them — that is, the deliverables. Sure, they are interested to some degree in the work performed but only as an indication that you are producing deliverables on a regular basis. The question to project managers then becomes: how should they orient their project plans? The answer should be obvious: orient your plan consistent with the client's interest. After all, the client is paying the bill. The switch from an activity orientation to a deliverable orientation is not that difficult if you are just starting in project management. However, if you have always begun your project's plan as activities, then this first step might prove difficult. Experience tells us that even the hardiest of "activity-based project managers" readily will see the value and quickly can adapt to this new way of thinking, approaching, and orienting their project plans. An open mind to a new way of looking at the project will facilitate greatly this transition. Stand by to be converted.

## All Projects Have Physical Deliverables

Experience will tell us that all projects, no matter how ethereal, have physical deliverables. A project to improve an organization's morale has deliverables. A project to improve the company's market position has deliverables. A project to reconstruct a school curriculum has deliverables. A project to reorganize a staff has deliverables. A project to conduct a meeting has deliverables. All human efforts have deliverables — that is what we do. Your task is to find the deliverables for your project. What do deliverables look like? That is the essence of Step 1.

If you are still not convinced that there are always project deliverables, then let us analyze an activity. An activity, as defined in project management literature and software, is a sentence consisting of "an action verb" and a subject. A subject consists of a noun or noun phrase. An example is: "Write requirements document." In this example, "Write" is the action verb and "requirements document" is the subject (the object). The subject consists of the noun (document) and a modifier (requirements). Therein, an activity must have a subject for it to be complete. The subject is the deliverable of the action verb, "Write." The natural conclusion is that as you define an activity, you always define a deliverable. Are you now convinced that projects always have physical deliverables? Maybe now you can see that you have always been defining the deliverable first.

## The Best Source of Deliverables

Part One of this book laid out the possible sources for a definition of the project's deliverables. The best source is still the client's own words. This can take many forms — the best format is a written definition. This does not say that other documents are not good sources of deliverable definitions; it only says that if you have a client-based document, it should be your guiding principle in the definition of your project. A written document of some form is the basis for Step 1.

## Expectations

If you delve into what a project manager manages, you will find that we manage expectations. The clients' expectations are everything. Again, they pay the bill and it is only right that they get what they pay for. The clients' written document represents the first level of their expectations. Be careful when discussing with your client their expectations; do not tell them that you "are managing their expectations" (although you really are). Managing their expectations speaks to managing and controlling them; you cannot control another person. The terminology you need to adopt is that you are "managing *to* their expectation." It is all in the "*to*."

## Just-In-Time (JIT) Training
### Use the Client's Words Only

Because we are using a written document as our source of deliverables, we need to be strict in its use. Whatever the source of the document, use *only the words in the document* — the client's own words. The reason is that in the next step we will be reviewing the project deliverables with the client. The last thing you want to happen during this presentation is a discussion over what the words (now displayed as deliverables) mean to the client — hopefully they will recognize and understand their own words. Consistent with this instruction is a second recommendation: neither make their words into an acronym nor abbreviate them. Acronyms and abbreviations will always require further untimely discussion. You need to control the presentation and any such discussion may cause you to lose control.

## Do Not Add Any Deliverables, Even If You Know They Are Missing

As you search the documents, you will find where deliverables have been "missed." Your first inclination will be to fill in the missing deliverables — fight the urge for now. Any added deliverables at this step could lead to difficulties during your upcoming client presentation, and the fact that they are missing will be useful during your presentation; more on this point in Step 2. As you find missing deliverables, make careful note of the fact for use in Step 2 and Step 3.

## Find the Deliverables — Nouns Only

We have already discussed what component of English syntax represents a deliverable — that is, a noun. What you will be looking for during your document search is the nouns; they are potentially the project's deliverables. You can highlight them with the highlighter pens or underline them. If the noun has a modifier (adjective), also include it. Not all nouns represent a project deliverable. In most cases, ignore any "proper noun"— for example, "Mr. James" or "The First National Bank." In addition, you need to test whether a particular noun is really a project deliverable *in this case*— for example, "research committee," "unit morale," or "higher profits." These may be deliverables in some projects but are they in this particular project?

If there is any doubt, then include the noun (deliverable) and question your client as to its true meaning when you make your client presentation.

In English (and particularly in American technical English), there is the tendency to take a verb and turn it into a noun — a gerund. As an example, "Writing is easy." In this usage, "writing" is the verb but it implies a deliverable — "a writing." You will need to test each such word that looks like a verb but in usage is really a noun — a deliverable. This process of finding the deliverables is much like a treasure hunt — they can be hidden anywhere.

## *Write Out the Post-Its®*

As you find a noun that you think is a deliverable, write it on a 3 × 3-inch Post-It. Write one Post-It for each deliverable; and if it is a noun clause, write the entire clause (Figure 5.1).

This format is not a "standard" by any means. Any form at this time will be fine as long as the writing is legible and clear from a short distance (four to

> Employee's
> Program

**Figure 5.1   3 × 3-inch Post-It.**

six feet). Do not be concerned that multiple documents will produce duplicate Post-Its; duplicates will become evident and eliminated in Step 2.

# Let's Practice: Step 1

We can use the case study to practice. Your assignment of this special event happens very simply by a note from your boss (Figure 5.2). This note was all you had to start the project. Your boss is the head of research and he wants you to plan a one-day recognition event.

> Provide a recognition event for 400 employees and their families with programs for adults and children all on one day.

**Figure 5.2   A note from your boss.**

Now circle the deliverables he has described thus far (Figure 5.3). Not much here, but it is a beginning. Now look at some meeting notes you made a few days later (Figure 5.4). This document is beginning to reveal the client's expectations. Now highlight the additional deliverables he has just described (Figure 5.5).

This was a good start, but now we need more definition for the employees and spouses. The next day you meet and document that meeting (Figure 5.6).

> Provide a recognition event for 400 employees and their families with programs for adults and children all on one day.

**Figure 5.3   Circle the deliverables.**

Meeting Notes:
Wednesday 5th.

Boss: "I would like good safe programs for the employee's children. There seems to be three categories; teenagers, grade-schoolers, and the very young (maybe even babies).

The teenagers seem interested in only electronic games.

The grade-schooler would probably like physical activities such as event rides and games of skills.

The small children, well, they need to be cared for so their parents can attend the technical program, I guess that's a nursery.

Let's concentrate on defining these (programs) at this time. Let's meet during lunch tomorrow–to discuss the program for the adults.

**Figure 5.4    Some meeting notes.**

Now find the added deliverables (Figure 5.7) — some are hiding! You highlight "spouses" as a noun but upon further analysis, you decide that "spouses" is not a deliverable. This is the general process of finding and evaluating the project's deliverables. You now finish Step 1 by writing out a Post-It for each highlighted deliverable.

Meeting Notes:
Wednesday 5th.

Boss: "I would like good safe programs for the employee's children. There seems to be three categories; teenagers, grade-schoolers, and the very young (maybe even babies).

The teenagers seem interested in only electronic games.

The grade-schooler would probably like physical activities such as event rides and games of skills.

The small children, well, they need to be cared for so their parents can attend the technical program, I guess that's a nursery.

Let's concentrate on defining these (programs) at this time. Let's meet during lunch tomorrow–to discuss the program for the adults.

**Figure 5.5    Highlight the additional deliverables.**

Meeting Notes:
Thursday

Boss: " Let me tell you what I envision for the employee's program and to a much lesser degree the general entertainment.

Let's show off our latest patents and how they are helping the bottom line–demonstrations of how they are applied. You pick several of the more significant ones. The demonstration area will have to have special access security n– employees only.

While we are on that subject–the entire area must have access control and safety officers in the parking areas.

I want your recommendations on a program for the spouses and food service next week.

The entertainment must be first rate. You know I particularly like country western BUT not everyone does. Find a musical group that can cover them all.

**Figure 5.6   The next day you meet (notes).**

Meeting Notes:
Thursday

Boss: "Let me tell you what I envision for the employee's program and to a much lesser degree the general entertainment.

Let's show off our latest patents and how they are helping the bottom line–demonstrations of how they are applied. You pick several of the more significant ones. The demonstration area will have to have special access security n– employees only.

While we are on that subject–the entire area must have access control and safety officers in the parking areas.

I want your recommendations on a program for the spouses and food service next week.

The entertainment must be first rate. You know I particularly like country western BUT not everyone does. Find a musical group that can cover them all.

**Figure 5.7   Find the added deliverables.**

## Specific Facilitation Instructions

Any specific facilitation instructions will depend on who is involved in finding the deliverables. If you and you alone are performing Step 1, then the points under JIT training will suffice. If you involve others, you first will need to accept the rationale of first finding the deliverables. Then apply the training provided in JIT. How you handle this as a team effort will depend a great deal on your style and the number of persons involved. Between the two sections above and the "Let's Practice" section that followed, you should find the needed background and training.

## *Hints*

### *Many Documents*

If there are many documents, you must be prepared to refer to them as the source of each deliverable. Experience tells us that you can write the source for each deliverable on its Post-It (Figure 5.8). This hint can be a particular "lifesaver" if you are challenged about a deliverable's source — and you will be challenged. Simply give each document a letter (A, B, etc.) and the reference is simple. A deliverable from document "B", page 12, paragraph 4 is "B/12/4." A few challenges and a quick response on your part will eliminate any further challenges.

**Figure 5.8   Write the source.**

## *Different Types (Colors) of Post-Its®*

It is possible that you will have deliverables that could use some special designation. The case where the client has some deliverables is a good example. Experience tells us that a different color Post-It will provide that distinction. This is particularly powerful during the client presentation in Step 2. A "shocking pink" Post-It will stand out clearly from the normal yellow Post-Its and will probably cause a reaction from the client — "What is the significance of the pink Post-It?" This gives you a clear opening to discuss the client's contributions to the deliverable set — do not miss this opportunity.

### Do Not Be Concerned with Duplicates

As discussed above, do not be concerned that you might be producing duplicate Post-Its — Step 2 will eliminate them.

### A Good Method for Analyzing

This first step is a good method for analyzing documents, contracts, statements-of-work, agreements, and requirement documents. It provides a disciplined approach that takes a great deal of data and turns it into information.

### Be as Neat as Possible

The Post-Its should be written out as neatly as possible. The felt-tipped pens are probably your best instrument for clear, visible presentation media. You might have an urge to enter this information into a PC format of some sort — fight that urge. The deliverables at this stage must be in a format and medium that can be changed easily, and Post-Its provide just such a medium.

# Chapter 6

# Step 2

# *Build and Review the Initial Product Breakdown Structure (PBS)*

## Background (Build)

This step comprises two parts: (1) building the initial PBS (product breakdown structure) and (2) the presentation of your initial PBS to the client.

### *The Top Component of the WBS*

Just as a reminder, the PBS is the top component of the WBS (Figure 6.1). It represents the deliverables of the project.

During Step 2, you will be taking the Post-Its® developed during Step 1 and "building" the PBS. There are two formats for a PBS: (1) an organizational chart format and (2) an outline format. The organizational chart format (Figure 6.2) provides the best visual format and one quickly grasped by a new viewer, while the outline format (Figure 6.3) is a textual version of a PBS, which most people learned about in eighth-grade English class.

Project management copied the organizational chart format from Industrial Engineering — Industrial Engineering calls it a Gozinto chart and uses it to describe how to assemble a large object from its components.

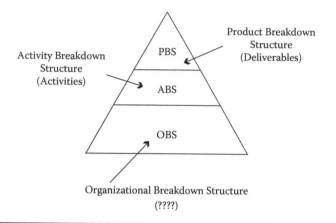

**Figure 6.1    Earliest version of WBS.**

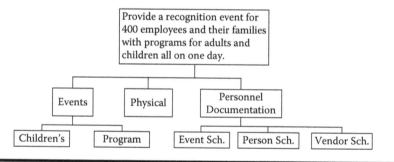

**Figure 6.2    The organizational chart.**

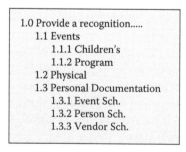

**Figure 6.3    The outline format.**

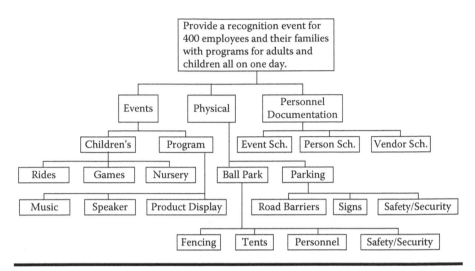

**Figure 6.4  Topmost level deliverable.**

In project management, it provides the same function; it shows how to assemble a project's deliverables into the final, topmost-level deliverable (Figure 6.4). Because of the visual aspects of the organizational format, it is the preferred format for Step 2. This visual will be presented to the client during this step and will result in an agreed-to set of project deliverables; most project managers recognize this set of deliverables as the "project's scope."

# JIT Training (Build)

## *The Initial Build of the PBS*

This step of the Process utilizes the Post-Its developed in Step 1 to build the initial PBS. The designation "initial PBS" means that this first PBS will represent only the beginning — that is, the initial version. In reality, the PBS is never "final." The PBS is a "living document," subject to change as needed and approved. There are many ways to build the PBS. There is no standard, generally accepted organization of any PBS. Its organization ultimately reflects the consensus of the project team.

During Step 2, the initial PBS will become the visual portion of the client presentation and will take on greater, more important meaning than what its DoD (Department of Defense) originators intended.

This step utilizes the organizational chart format and all further references to a PBS will mean the organizational chart format.

We speak of the *depth* of the PBS as the number of levels. The topmost deliverable is "level zero." The next level is the first level; the next level is second level, etc. (Figure 6.5). The importance of the levels is that they represent where all the

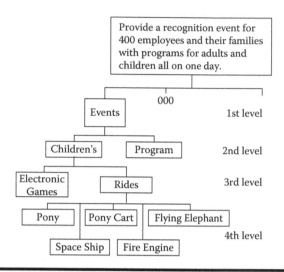

**Figure 6.5 Levels of deliverables.**

lower levels come together; some refer to this as the 100-percent principle (ref 1). The principle of 100 percent is that every level represents all the levels (deliverables) below it and in the same "leg." The term "leg" refers to the logical progression of superior to subordinate.

In Figure 6.5, the "Events" leg is the leftmost leg at the first level. At the next level below (second level), two legs ("Children's" and "Program") begin (i.e., split off). "Events" is the superior, and "Children's" and "Program" are its subordinates. Legs represent successively lower levels (detail) of deliverables.

## *A PBS Can Have Different Depths (Level of Detail)*

The number of levels will depend on the detail contained in the defining documents. Experience tells us that most initial PBSs will be very "shallow" — that is, not many levels. Initial PBSs also tend to be "wide" — that is, many legs. Frequently, a PBS will have greater depth in one leg. This usually indicates that one or more of the defining documents have extensive detail concerning one particular level (usually the first level). The result can be a lopsided PBS but this does not create a bad situation. If this condition should occur, it is an indication of some special meaning (importance) to the client. The client either might have a special interest or have very detailed special experience or knowledge of the deliverable. This should indicate an area where you too should develop a special interest.

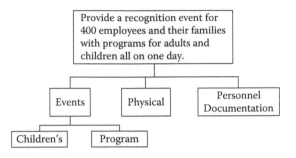

**Figure 6.6   Your initial PBS.**

As you build the PBS, you will quickly note where deliverables are missing. This is not the time to add deliverables not described in the original documents — remember the client's words only!

However, do not discard any deliverables that you consider missing; just set them aside for Step 3.

## Let's Practice: Part One

You decide how to organize the first level of your initial PBS (Figure 6.6). As you can see, there is very little depth but is does have some width. This organization will probably require some adjustments later. Once the first level is established, you can start assembling the PBS from the available defined deliverables (Figure 6.7).

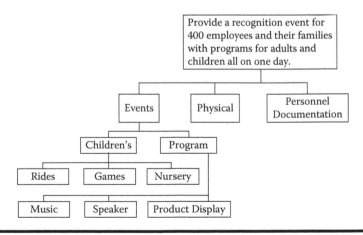

**Figure 6.7   Assembling the PBS.**

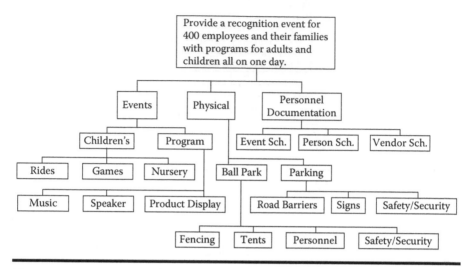

**Figure 6.8   A more complete form.**

Further meetings with your boss and event planners help define additional, more detailed deliverables. The initial PBS now takes on a more complete form (Figure 6.8).

## Specific Facilitation Instructions (Build)

As in Step 1, specific facilitation instructions will depend on whether you are involving others in your initial build effort. The specific instructions below should suffice for most alternatives.

## Build Your Working Surface

It is now time to build (assemble) the initial PBS. You will need a working surface. If you are working all by yourself and you believe the PBS will be reasonably small, then it can be contained on a large desktop. In this case, you might consider using a Post-It smaller than the 3 × 3 inch ones specified in the supplies list (see "Opening"). If you believe that the resulting PBS will be large (greater than 35 to 40 deliverables and more than six legs), then consider using a blank wall as your working surface. Your experience eventually will help you decide where to work. It is always easy to start small and move to a larger working surface. Once you have decided on the working surface, your need to cover it with either flipchart paper or banner paper. Covering the surface has two purposes: (1) to provide a "moveable" document and (2) to protect the original surface (you are going to draw lines between

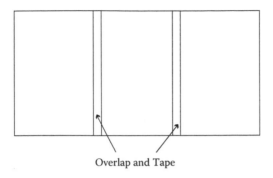

Overlap and Tape

**Figure 6.9   Use lots of masking tape.**

the Post-Its with felt-tipped pens). If you use flipchart paper, tape the seams of the pages together to make a contiguous piece of paper — use lots of masking tape (Figure 6.9).

It is important that the paper be contiguous to allow for easy movement of the PBS to the client's office.

## *Assemble the PBS*

The actual PBS organization is highly project specific and there cannot be a specific set of instructions. You will have to determine its order of assembly for yourself; remember that we are using the organizational chart format (Figure 6.10) for this step.

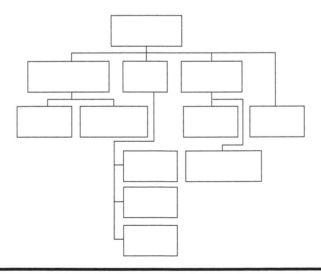

**Figure 6.10   Organizational chart format.**

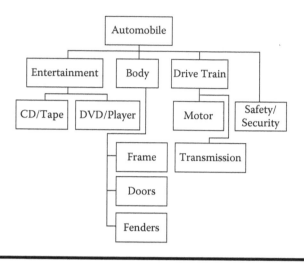

**Figure 6.11   The "Automobile" is the topmost deliverable.**

This example of a PBS shows four legs and a depth to the second level. The dot-dot on the right of the first level indicates there are more legs than can be displayed. If you look at a PBS of something very familiar to most us (see Figure 6.11), maybe it will help you understand how to assemble a PBS. The "Automobile" is the topmost deliverable (level zero). The first level consists of four legs: "Entertainment," "Body," "Drive Train," and "Safety/Security." It may look like the "Safety/ Security" deliverable is at third level but it is only drawn lower for ease of display (i.e., enough room). The lines from one level to the next will always dedicate its level (organizational relationship). The "Drive Train" is defined further at the second level by "Motor" and "Transmission." The "Body" is defined at the second level by "Frame" and "Doors." Of course, one of the most important first-level deliverables is "Entertainment." It is further decomposed at the second level by "CD/Tape" and "DVD/Player." The possible variations on this theme are endless. Your first task is to find the topmost deliverable for the project. This topmost deliverable is probably what the client calls "the project." You may find it highlighted either in a document (in capitals or boldface) or in some special organization of the documents. If your search does not seem to reveal what the client calls the project, then give it a name of your own and proceed. You should be able to clear the issue of the project name during the upcoming client presentation. Now that the zero level (project name) is initially established, you need to determine the natural organization of the PBS. Do not linger very long on the first level. Experience tells us that the first level's organization is important, but it will change many times during the Process.

## *Hints (Build)*

### *Ready to Go?*

You have completed what you consider the initial PBS. Are you ready for the client presentation?

Your PBS assembly must take into consideration the mechanics of the presentation. If you have used the larger Post-Its and banner paper, then it might be difficult to transport over a long distance. You might consider the smaller format of $1 \times 1\frac{1}{2}$-inch Post-Its. In this case, consider using display boards. Display boards are available at office supply firms and are used by schools for portable displays at science fairs. If possible, use the $3 \times 3$-inch Post-Its because they remain the easiest to view from a distance. Another consideration is the sheer number of deliverables. If you have more than 75 deliverables, the smaller Post-Its might be best. Large numbers of deliverables in the $3 \times 3$-inch size will create large charts with handling, transportation, and display problems. But do not let this scare you — you will handle whatever you decide.

### *PC Software or Not?*

About now, you might be considering whether to use some PC software to record the PBS — fight that urge. The Post-It and a hand-drawn PBS is your best medium for the client presentation. It shows your work and it is portable. Most importantly, it can be quickly changed and added to. This decision will be vital during your client presentation.

## Background (Review)

The second part of this step is preparation for and making the client presentation (subsequently called the Presentation). The ultimate objective of the Presentation is to obtain the client's buy-in to the PBS's organization. A secondary objective would be to establish a base for future communications regarding project progress.

Before you are ready, further analysis needs to happen. The source documents may not reveal the total deliverables the client is considering. Usually, there are more deliverables than the documents have revealed. If anyone else has been involved with the client regarding the project, you need to involve him or her in a pre-presentation review. Any extra involvement by others can establish expectations (additional deliverables) not contained in any document, and you need to know these expectations before you talk with the client. This pre-presentation review also will give you another person's perspective of your PBS's organization. If anyone in your line of authority (your manager) has been involved, this is the time to get their buy-in to your PBS. If your organization is extensive and therefore several pre-presentations may be required — additional time must be set aside. This series of meetings may be necessary to get your organization fully aligned with your project but also should help reduce delays later on due to misunderstandings, etc. This presentation series also can reveal a great deal about your organization's perception of your project and help identify any possible future support difficulties within your own organization.

The Presentation itself has many advantages. One is to reveal just who is your client. Frequently, a project manager is not clear just who is the principal client. The principal client is that person who will take your progress reports, initiate client change requests, and help you decide what changes to implement.

There is another point regarding the Presentation — it is not necessary at this time. However, a presentation of the PBS to your client needs to happen, and it needs to happen *before* you begin the project. Some project managers prefer to hold a PBS review after the planning session (for their own reasons). Experience tells us that the Presentation will reveal much about the project (deliverables) and the client (expectations) that is immediately useable during the planning session. If you delay the Presentation until after the Session, any new information could require considerable re-planning — not a popular action with your project team.

## JIT Training (Review)

If you are experienced in presentations, there will be little new knowledge added here. However, before you can make a successful presentation, you must assure yourself that your own understanding and acceptance of these basic principles (may be new to you) are complete. Any hesitation on your part regarding the PBS will be easily "read" by your client. If this should occur, it could cause considerable harm to your credibility.

Key to your presentation is your explanation of the PBS. If your client has experience with the PBS, you need only explain (1) how you have organized the project and (2) the source (or sources) of the deliverables. You probably will not need to explain the concept of deliverables to the client, but it would not hurt to remind them — as deliverables are the client's only interest.

If the client is unfamiliar with the concepts of deliverables and the PBS, you should assume their full interest and proceed with a complete explanation.

## Let's Practice: Part Two

You prepare by explaining the initial PBS to several persons. These advance presentations provided you with notes that are indicative of any presentation gaps (quality of your presentation), their interest (proper depth of your presentation), and their lack of understanding (clarity of your presentation). Your notes help you further refine your presentation by getting you "out ahead" of possible similar questions at the Presentation.

---

## Specific Facilitation Instructions (Review)

No specific facilitation instructions are necessary.

---

## Hints (Review)

### Upon Arrival

Upon arriving at the client's site, your first action will be to determine where you can display your initial PBS. Be sure to ask your client's permission before attaching it to any wall. As soon as you are ready, try to either move your client closer or even stand in front of the PBS. This will help you achieve the objectives of the presentation.

## Objectives of the Presentation

The presentation has several objectives:

1. Exchange information about the project
2. Gain your client's buy-in and
3. Explain how you will be reporting progress.

The first objective is to exchange information, and there can be many questions needing answers from both sides of the communication process.

The objective of client buy-in is essential to your ultimate success. You will need some indication or signal from the client that he or she has bought in to the project as defined by the PBS. What you need is an action on his or her part indicating understanding and agreement. Experience tells us that a simple trick might just make that happen. The buy-in process really starts as soon as you arrive. The client will instantly see the PBS as "yours." However, you want the presentation to end with the PBS becoming "ours" — that is, gaining buy-in. As long as the client never touches the PBS, it will remain "yours." You need something to make clients engage with the PBS and make it "theirs."

## Play a Little Trick

Before arriving, rearrange the PBS to make it *imperfect* by either moving a deliverable, losing a deliverable, or adding a nonsensical deliverable. As soon as the clients see this obvious error, they will point it out to you. This gives you the opportunity to "play dumb." Immediately offer the client a pad of Post-Its and a marker, and ask the client to add, modify, or change the PBS "as they see it." If you can get the client to perform this task, the whole question of "Who owns the PBS?" can change.

In addition, the client's personal pronoun can "give away" their attitude regarding the PBS. When you start the presentation, their pronouns (regarding the PBS) are usually "you," "yours," or "it." When they feel the PBS is now "theirs," they change their pronouns to "we" and "ours." It works every time! Frequently, a tactual person will reveal their feeling regarding the PBS by simply touching it. If you see this happen, "you have them" — it is theirs!

## *Progress Reporting Style*

The third objective is your description of how you will be reporting project progress. Because deliverables are the bases for the project, they should be the subject of your progress report. Explain to your client that the PBS will be the medium for your progress reports. Describe that when the project begins, you will be posting (with their permission) a copy of the full PBS in an area of their choice. Then as each deliverable starts, you will be marking the PBS to this fact (Figure 6.12).

A line drawn from the upper left corner to the bottom right corner of the Post-It signifies a started deliverable. Then when the deliverable is completed, a second line drawn from the upper right to the bottom left corner will form an "X" and signify a completion (Figure 6.13). Explain that, in this manner, he or she will have a visual progress record.

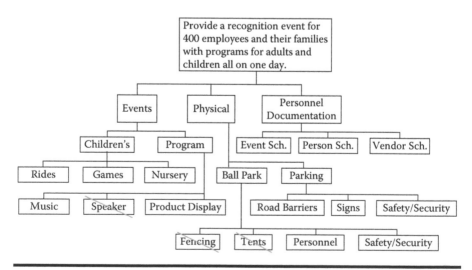

**Figure 6.12   A line will signify a start.**

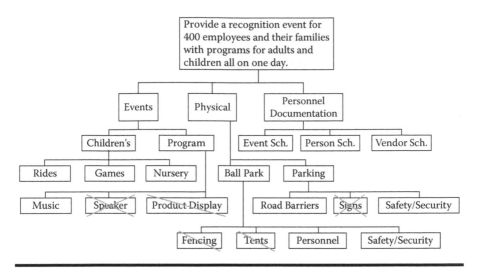

**Figure 6.13 An "X" will signify completion.**

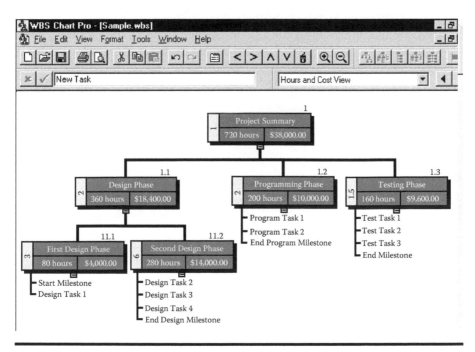

**Figure 6.14 WBS Chart Pro™.**

## Other Display Techniques

A difficulty with any wallchart is its lasting power in an office environment. Long-term exposure will cause Post-Its to fall off, curl up, and eventually turn other colors. There are alternatives to long-term usage of Post-Its. One such alternative is a PC product, WBS Chart Pro™ — obtained from the Web site Criticaltools.com (for example, see Figure 6.14)

This PC software produces the PBS (in organizational format) from many different printers. In addition, it has input directly into MS Project™ — you do not have to input your data a second time. Experience tells us that your PBS will appear much more professional in a large-scale, plastic-coated format. Several nationwide office supply stores can produce your PBS directly from your WBSCHART™ data files and then plastic-coat it for a longer life.

# Chapter 7

# Step 3
# Building Down the PBS

## Background

The PBS (project breakdown structure) at the end of Step 2 is really just a "skeleton of a project body." The build-down of the PBS is simply adding further deliverables to make up a full deliverables set. In keeping with a body analogy, it adds the muscle, flesh, etc. The build-down step was added, after noting in repeated Step 4 sessions that at the beginning there was a period of little or no progress (plan development). The slow-down phenomenon was due to the lack of sufficient deliverables to plan the project. The addition of the build-down step before Step 4 and before the full planning team was deployed solved this problem.

In short, the PBS build-down provides a "kick-start" for the planning session in terms of how the project manager wants the activities developed and sends a clear message of his or her management style.

## JIT Training

### Successive Decomposition

The basis for the build-down process is the concept of successive decomposition. The original deliverables are decomposed into increasingly smaller and smaller subcomponents (they are displayed as lower levels on the same leg). The build-down also provides a clear message concerning the activity granularity (size of an activity).

## A Question of Granularity

The question of granularity always surfaces during Step 4 (activities). As result of the build-down, the lowest level of the PBS settles this question. Past attempts to establish a consistency of durations has resulted in policy statements such as "no activity shall have duration greater than 40 hours." This arbitrary statement is not appropriate in a project driven by deliverables; each activity defines the *complete* delivery of a deliverable. An arbitrary 40 hours can only cause either partial deliverables or ones "made up" to match the 40 hours. Any "made up" deliverables (to comply with such a statement) only degrade the quality of the progress reporting process.

## Approaches for the Build-Down

There are three approaches to the build-down:

1. Your effort alone
2. A combination of you and SMEs (subject matter experts)
3. The full planning team at the beginning of Step 4

A build-down normally uses one of the first two approaches. The full team approach will increase the time needed for Step 4 but does have a clear advantage in providing *de facto* team buy-in — *if they build it, it is theirs.*

## Client's Deliverables

A well-defined PBS has three components. The client provides the "client's deliverables" to the project. These deliverables vary: documents, work-site faculties, access to areas and documents, money, etc. A different color Post-It will highlight the client's deliverables. A separate dedicated PBS leg also will help to highlight them.

## Process Deliverables

The second deliverable type is the process deliverable. These deliverables are related to the project development process itself (process deliverables). They can amount to 25 percent of your project workload. Process deliverables are simply the "glue components" of a project. Process deliverables are not necessarily delivered to the client but the project deliverables cannot be delivered without them. They usually take the form of written documents — a process, a specification, a strategy, an inventory, etc. There is always a question of where on the PBS do you place process deliverables. There seems to be two styles. One style (scattered deliverables) places the process deliverable on the PBS leg related to it; for example, "the refreshment contract" would be on the "refreshment leg." This works fine until a process deliverable involves multiple legs, such as "tenting specifications." Experience tells us that scattered process deliverables are sometimes difficult to find. A better solution is to gather them together on a PBS leg of their own. This style (grouped) provides quick access to the process deliverables.

## Project Deliverables to the Fourth Level

The ideal lowest level for project deliverables is the fourth level (Figure 7.1). The DoD (U.S. Department of Defense) calls this "the manager's level of control."

This fourth level is the level where there is sufficient information to control the project and manage the project team. Any further definition (levels) would approach the point of "micro managing" the project team. There are exceptions to the fourth level as the lowest level needed. When any deliverable is subcontracted is one exception. In this case, the subcontractor must define two additional levels of deliverable below the subcontracted item. This provides additional information for managing the subcontractor. The second exception is when a deliverable is an unknown to your project team. In this case, additional levels of definition will ultimately be required — not necessarily now, but soon. Two more exceptions are related to the team members: (1) where a team member is an unknown to the project manager, more levels needed; and (2) where the member is very familiar and very reliable, fewer levels are needed. The implication of fewer or more levels is the amount of activities that will result and the size (duration) of the activity. You will see this implication more clearly in Step 4. Another reason for the build-down is to provide consistency with regard to the size of resulting activities (Step 4).

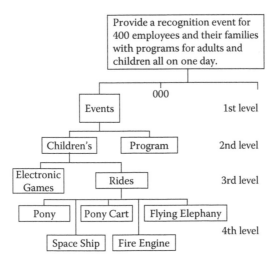

**Figure 7.1   The fourth level.**

If you can achieve consistency (to the same level) for the majority of the PBS, the resulting activities will have similar durations.

## Sources for More Detailed Deliverables

There can be other sources for more detailed deliverables: previous projects of your own, lesson learned documents, standard templates (expected deliverables), and contracts from previous or similar projects. Many organizations do maintain just such files. Lacking any such file organization, you will be on your own.

## Exceptions

There may be other categories of deliverables. One such proposed category is "new technology deliverables." If you are working in a technology with a high number of new technologies, just such a category may exist for you. You would want such a category on your PBS as a "place keeper." The development of its deliverables would then be a "work in progress" and would warrant a PBS leg of its own.

### Let's Practice

You are just back from the Presentation and a number of deliverables were further defined (Figure 7.2).

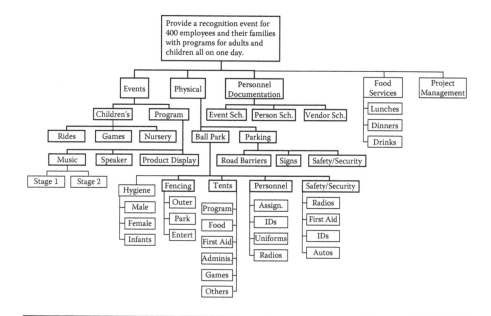

**Figure 7.2   More deliverables defined.**

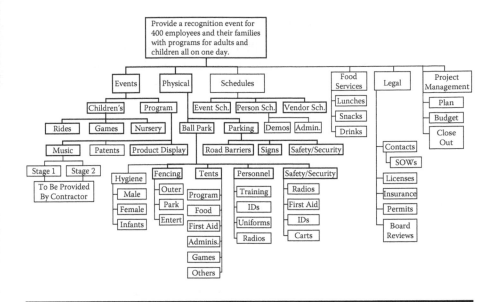

**Figure 7.3 You eliminated several items.**

Your planning session starts in two days and you want more deliverables to "fill out" the PBS. Your history search turns up last year's event project manager and you engage him for an hour as an SME. During that meeting, you eliminated several items from the PBS and add a few more (Figure 7.3).

At this point, you have expended your detail knowledge and you are ready to bring on the full project team. The definition of the deliverables is, in most legs, to the fourth level. There were no *client deliverables,* and more than half of the defined deliverables are *process deliverables.* The large content of process deliverables seems justified for a project at this level of detail. It was difficult at times to remember the definition of your assignment, "The project plan is to include only the planning portion and not the actual implementation of the event." The assignment, as defined, is to include deliverables only to the point of starting the event. Thereafter, the individual vendors and implementation teams will be in full control (with their own plans).

## Hints

The Client Need Not See the Process Deliverables

The process deliverables normally are not part of the project deliverables. However, many times there are process deliverables that will be of value to the client — for example, inventories, layout diagrams, lists of personnel required, timing charts for events, etc. In this case, they are considered "value added" to the client and should be made available.

## The PBS Is a Work in Progress-

You and your team need to consider the PBS as a work in progress — a living document. Maintain this attitude throughout the project and the PBS will continue as a visual representation of the project's status, scope, and organization. For this to happen, the entire team must see it as a living document. More on this later (Steps 4 through 7).

## Show Your Work: Leave It on Post-Its®

If your team members are computer oriented, they will probably have the urge to take the content on the Post-Its into computer graphics. The Post-Its are not only for planning; they can be your total tool (media) for representing your project in many ways. Unless your project will occur over a long time period, the Post-It will suffice for all presentations and management actions (planning, control, and execution). Experience tells us that PC software is not needed for all projects. This point will be reinforced in Part Three, Chapter 14 ("Manual Scheduling").

## The Project Management Leg®

Although seldom specified, there should always be a project management leg. Most project management deliverables are not delivered to your client. If you keep track of the total project effort and the project management content of that effort, you will find that project management deliverables will represent between 12 and 20 percent of the total project effort. This alone is sufficient reason to include a project management leg on the PBS.

## Issues/Problems/Risks

All during the Process, your team will surface project difficulties. In the English language, these difficulties have many names (terms): issues, problems, risks, etc. Experience tells us to define our terms. Some suggested definitions would be:

- A *problem* is something the project team can resolve (it is within their control).
- An *issue* is something the project manager must resolve (it is beyond the control of the team).
- A *risk* is a difficulty that can be defined and perhaps managed as the project proceeds.

## *The Parking Lot*

Experience tells us to record these "difficulties," no matter what they are called. Some difficulties can be resolved during the planning session, while others cannot. The unresolvable difficulties can be set aside for later resolution. This concept of "setting aside" is called "a parking lot." Post-Its are a good medium for recording these unresolved items.

If this is a new idea for your organization, define it for them and create a *parking lot* (on a flipchart). It is best if you control the parking lot by overseeing its input of unresolved items — so that you will understand them and know their origins (i.e., who defined it).

## *An Assumption*

There will be difficulties that can be resolved, but only with a stated assumption. The definition of assumption for our purposes is a statement considered true until proven otherwise. As with "parking lot difficulties," you need to record planning assumptions. Another flipchart will facilitate this mechanism and, as with the parking lot, you need to control its input.

# Chapter 8

## Step 4
## Establishing the Activities

## Background

### Most Project Managers Start Here

Most project managers start their project planning with activities (Step 4). However, there is a small but growing segment of project managers starting first with deliverables (Step 1). Experience tells us that the switch to deliverables is not difficult for a beginning project manager, but the switch can be very difficult for an experienced one. Most people think of "what they have to do" rather than "what they will achieve." If the project manager deploys any kind of technology team, this difficulty is reinforced by the team's tendency toward considering activities first.

Experience tells us after many times "at bat" to begin the project planning session with your PBS (product breakdown structure) will start off the planning team and the session in the right way.

### Their Time Is Yours

There may be a tendency on the part of some project managers to limit the interaction of the project team — "they are busy people and it might interfere with their work." If this is your attitude, you will need to reconsider their role versus yours in project planning. Your team members are the best source of knowledge about the project and they have the skills to fulfill the project's objectives — this is their role! If you are just beginning as a project manager or you are trying out the participatory approach to planning, you need to adopt the attitude of "their time is yours" — you need their knowledge. You only move the project forward through their labors and you cannot be timid.

## Time Boxed

Each of the remaining steps of the Process should be "time boxed." Time boxed means that a time period is set aside and maintained as best you can. There are steps that easily will exceed the time period. They will run out of time because either the step is not complete or no one is satisfied with the results. When extra time is required, you will know.

## Are You Ready?

Your personal preparation, the site preparations, and your timing need considerable organization for this step. As part of your personal preparation, you need to think through each action of the step to ensure that you understand what is to be done and why. Hopefully, the background portion of each step will prepare you. Your preparation and the PBS are the bases for this team-oriented step.

## JIT Training

### Establishing Your Authority and Delegating It

It is not possible to tell you how exactly to conduct this step but the key will be you establishing your leadership. A charter is a document that defines your authority and how you are held accountable. It is an excellent leadership tool. During the session, you are essentially delegating your authority by assigning deliverables to specific individuals. Any assignment (delegation) includes defining the activities that will produce the deliverable and reporting their status and completion (accountability). An assignment made is a *de facto* delegation of your authority.

Experience tells us that a formal statement (as follows) can make the delegation clear:

> "As you know, I am the project manager and I realize only you will complete the project. Therefore, I am delegating to you the authority to define the deliverables and the activities that will produce them. I, in turn, will hold you accountable for your actions and their results."

The first time you recite this statement, they will be surprised.

## Restate the Project's Purpose

You will need to restate the purpose of the project. The PBS is the perfect medium for this presentation. If your team has no experience with the PBS, you may need to explain it — they quickly will grasp its meaning and organization.

## How Much to Plan

Before the session begins, "how much to plan" is another issue you need to settle. It is like the old adage, "How do you eat an elephant? ... One bite at a time." If your project is longer than three months, it may not be reasonable to plan the entire project at this time. In this case, you need to consider what would be a natural timeframe for refreshing the project plan. In any long-term project, there exists a "window of knowledge." This window is a fact requiring your attention and a decision. Whether or not you establish a plan to conduct a refresh, you will need to refresh the project plan. There will come a day when your plan does not have sufficient information to control the project and manage the team — that is, you have reached the end of the "window of knowledge." Experience tells us that a 12-month project will require three or four plan refreshes. The concept of planned refreshes is based on the "folded map" approach (Figure 8.1) to long-term project planning.

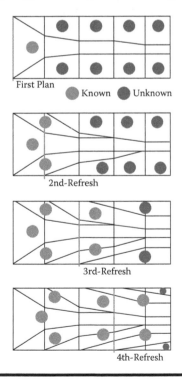

Figure 8.1   The "folded map."

The "first plan" gathers all known activities (the "known" in Figure 8.1) within a reasonable timeframe (your window of knowledge) plus any key activities happening out in time. The "2nd Refresh" adds to the project knowledge (plan), as do the "3rd" and "4th Refresh." In this manner, you only plan the activities that you know about in your window of knowledge and you conduct plan refreshes at set times. If the project has "phases," they would be a good point for refreshing the project plan. Another natural, initial segment could be if you expect there will be considerable initial effort to define an approach, discover a process, investigate or select vendors, etc. In any of these situations, you need forethought concerning how much you will plan for the Session — how big of a bite will you take?

## Assembly Points

There are always more activities than deliverables because (1) a deliverable may require several activities, and (2) there are activities not associated to a deliverable. These latter special activities are associated to the assembly of multiple deliverables into the next-higher deliverable. This can occur each time the lower-level deliverables of a leg combine at the next level (an assembly point; Figure 8.2).

Figure 8.2 depicts where assembly point activities can occur. They tend to be activities related to quality, integration, testing, and client interactions (review, acceptance, etc.). Team members define and execute assembly point activities at the lower levels but those at the topmost levels are either executed or facilitated by the project manager.

## Gaining Team Buy-In

The Session has two main purposes: (1) to understand whether your project team can actually complete the project on the target endpoint (validate the endpoint) and (2) to gain the team's buy-in (commitment). The Process will provide the first

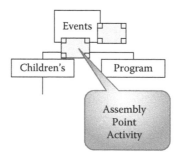

**Figure 8.2   An assembly point.**

purpose (i.e., validation) by virtue of the methods used. The second purpose (buy-in) will require some special effort on your part. As with your client, you need some specific action that signifies the team's buy-in. You could simply ask them whether they buy in, but would you really get a true answer? There is no recognized method of gaining the needed buy-in. Project managers develop their own style concerning this issue.

Experience tells us that the trick you played on your client also might work here. Before your team arrives, make the PBS's organization either incomplete, incorrect, or just plain silly. Remove a few deliverables (Post-Its®) that are in every project — the team will expect them. Add a few that do not make sense being in this project. Move Post-Its where they should not be — but do not be too obvious. When your team comes into the planning room, give them a few minutes to absorb the organization of the PBS. If they are experienced with the PBS, they will be looking for their deliverables. Then ask the entire team to gather around the PBS and begin your explanation of how you organized it. At this moment, the PBS is "yours." It will not be long before someone will ask, "Is this the organization you want the PBS to have?" Play dumb: "Yes, is there some trouble with its organization?" They then will readily admit that they think it is not perfect. When that happens, quickly hand out 3 x 3-inch Post-Its, felt-tipped pens, and step away from the PBS. They will proceed to make it "just right." It might even be back to the PBS that you made "un-right." This little trick can change their attitude — the PBS is now "theirs." If you cannot get them to change it, it will always be "yours" and buy-in will not occur. When a team feels the PBS is theirs, they touch it, change it, and generally rearrange it until they are satisfied — and "then it is theirs and you have them!"

## Let's Practice

You start the Session by reviewing the PBS from Step 3. In general, the team agrees with the items but not necessarily the PBS's organization (you really did not expect them to agree, did you?). After an hour, the team has made some minor rearrangements and added several more deliverables (Figure 8.3).

They seem pleased with their work result and especially pleased with the resulting transfer of knowledge. It is evident to you: they have "bought-in" to their newly, rearranged PBS.

Next, you discuss the issue of their "window of knowledge." We consider the facts: (1) the project's overall duration is less than three months, and (2) they have detailed knowledge of the effort involved. Therefore, we decide to plan the entire project at this session and to refresh the plan only once — two weeks before the event.

You passed out supplies, gave the necessary instructions, and then stood back. Their resulting activities were "posted" on the newly rearranged PBS (Figure 8.4).

When all deliverables were "covered" by activities, we reviewed the possibility of missing deliverables. I instructed them on the concept of "assembly point

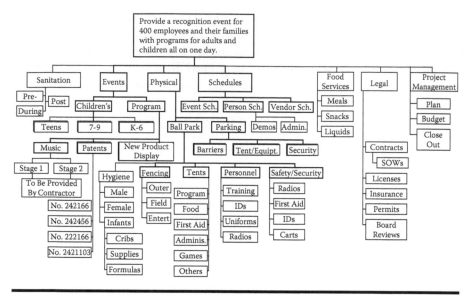

**Figure 8.3    Added several more deliverables.**

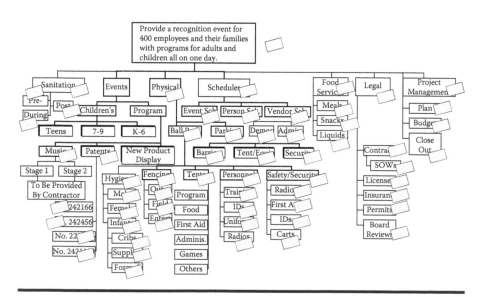

**Figure 8.4    Activities were "posted."**

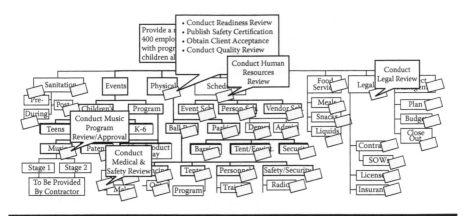

**Figure 8.5    Significant assembly points.**

activities" and, as expected, they found five significant assembly points that would require this type of activity (Figure 8.5).

The team defined the activities for the lower-level assembly points (there were four). You defined the four assembly point activities for the assembly of level-one components into level zero.

There still were some missing activities. Because the Children's Program was completely subcontracted, we decided to bring in that subcontractor — after some instruction, they will lay out their own plan (Figure 8.6).

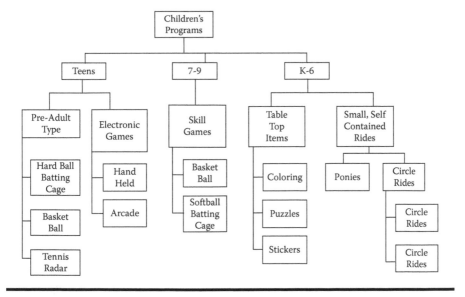

**Figure 8.6    Children's Program.**

After adding the vendor's project plan to our project plan, we amended their contract to include their reporting requirements.

## Specific Facilitation Instruction

This specific facilitation provides a script for instructing your team. If you are uncomfortable reading them, then simply paraphrase in your own words.

"Let me explain the entire Eight Step Process (Figure 8.7) and then I will lead you through each step, beginning with this — Step 4.

"In Step 1, I searched and found within the available documents, the project's deliverables. In Step 2, I developed this (pointing to your PBS), the initial Product Breakdown Structure (PBS). The PBS is a visual representation of the project deliverables; a simple example of a PBS is an Automobile PBS (Figure 8.8).

"A PBS displays how to assemble the topmost project deliverable ("Automobile") from lower-level components — it is essentially an assembly diagram. In the PBS, any one level represents the assembly of all the lower levels in the same leg. In Step 2, I took the PBS to our client and presented it for his approval.

"In Step 3, I and several other individuals worked to make the PBS more robust than the client had originally defined. The additional deliverables provided a more complete view of our project in terms of the project's deliverables. The PBS will ultimately contain three categories of deliverables: (1) the project deliverables, (2) any deliverables the client will provide, and (3) process deliverables. Process deliverables usually are documents. They define the sub-process of our overall management process (testing, acceptance, procedures, etc,); any tools we will use; any practice standards; etc. We will develop the process deliverable for our own use. We do not deliver process deliverables to the client

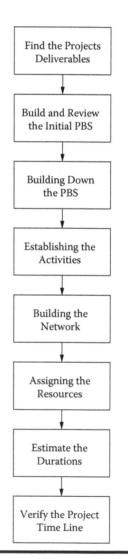

**Figure 8.7   The Eight Step Process.**

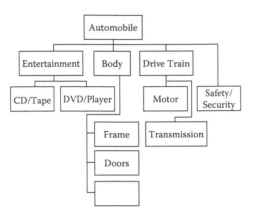

**Figure 8.8   An "Automobile" PBS.**

but we cannot deliver the project deliverables without them. Step 4 is where you (the planning team) will engage the project to build a project plan. During this step, you will review the PBS and make any adjustments that you see necessary — the PBS as it is now, is only my idea. Then you will use the PBS to develop your activities to produce the deliverables. During Step 5, you will assemble your activities in logical order (network) — timewise from left to right. During Step 6, you will add the resources required for each activity. During Step 7, you will get the first chance to estimate the duration of each of your activities. During Step 8 (final step), I will lead you through the process of validating the endpoint date for the project."

The Process sounds like a "straight fall-through;" it is not — it is an iterative process (Figure 8.9). You can see that there are several chances to return to previous steps to add deliverables, add activities, modify durations, and alter network logic. In this manner, we can keep the PBS as "a living document" of our project's deliverables content (the project's scope).

"In addition, after we have completed the first full pass, we will go back to Step 3 to add special activities and to reassess our durations. This return process is the Second Pass."

(Optional — if you want to deliver the authorization statement):

"As you know, I am the authorized project manager but I realize you will produce the project. Therefore, I am delegating to you the authority to define the deliverables and the activities that will produce them. I, in turn, will hold you accountable for your actions and their results."

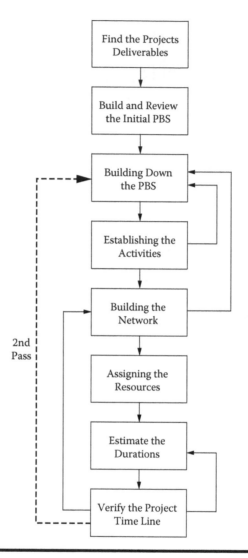

**Figure 8.9   An iterative process.**

"Now, let me give you instructions on Step 4: Establishing the activities. First, I want you to review the deliverables assigned. You should add additional deliverables as you see fit. When you are satisfied with the level of detail (lowest level) of the PBS, then we can begin developing your activities to produce the deliverable. You will need at least one activity per deliverable, but you can have multiple activities per deliverable. In an ideal sense, your lowest-level deliverable should be at the fourth level. You will see some of the deliverables are already defined to the fourth level and at this time, the fourth level is sufficient.

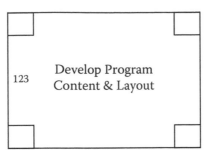

**Figure 8.10 Each activity has a unique identifier (UI).**

During our Second Pass through the Process, it may be necessary to define additional levels for your deliverables.

"We will be using these 3 × 5-inch Post-Its (hold up a pack) to write out our activities. Each Post-It will represent a deliverable. Please follow this format for your Post-Its. Write the activity's description in the center of the Post-It. Give each activity a unique identifier (UI) and write it to the left of the description. The UI is simply a whole number with at least three digits (suggest beginning with 100) (Figure 8.10). This number has no meaning other than a unique number for its activity (much more on the UI later). Also, please do not write in the boxes in the four corners; they are reserved for activities schedules. Use the felt-tipped pins provided and write your descriptions as neatly as possible — others will need to read them. The activity description is a complete sentence — a verb and a noun. The noun for your activity comes from the deliverable on the PBS. The verb is your choice. You need to use a verb that is appropriate for the noun and of a correct size. The concept of "size" was never part of your English lessons but it has meaning here. If your deliverable is "specification" (an example of a process deliverable), you can define it with either one or multiple activities. You can either use a series of activities with verbs such as, write, edit, print, hole punch, distribute, or you could have a single activity with a "large verb" such as "publish specification." In this context, the verb "publish" is a very "large verb." The verbs and the number of activities needed per deliverable are your choice. However, remember each activity you develop will become part of the project plan and will require your tracking and reporting (the accountability part of authority). Also, if the noun has a modifier (an adjective), include it on the Post-It. The activity description on the Post-Its should have both verb and noun — not just the verb.

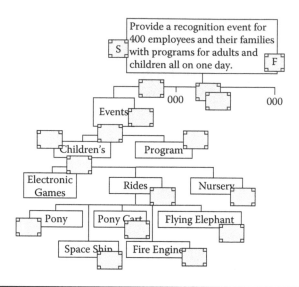

**Figure 8.11    Place the Post-Its over the deliverables.**

"When you have completed your Post-Its, place them over the deliverable (3 × 3-inch Post-It on the PBS) at either an angle or an offset (Figure 8.11).

"There is one more point before I let you start. There are always more activities than deliverables. There is of course the possibility you'll want to define several activities for a deliverable. There are other activities not directly associated to a deliverable but associated to the assembly of multiple deliverables into the next higher deliverable. This can occur each time the lower level deliverables of a leg are combined at the next level (an assembly point; Figure 8.12).

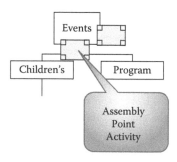

**Figure 8.12    An assembly point.**

"These activities describe assembly point activities. They tend to be activities related to quality, integration, testing, and client interactions (review, acceptance, etc.). Review each assembly point for this possibility and develop any necessary assembly point activities.

"Your review of the PBS and development of your activities might at any time reveal a missing deliverable. If this is the case, simply add the necessary deliverable to the PBS (Step 3) and then create an activity (Step 4) to produce the deliverable (Figure 8.13).

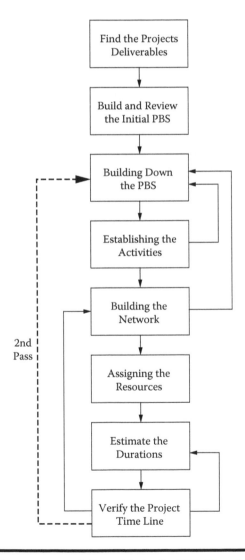

**Figure 8.13   Add the necessary deliverable to the PBS (Step 3).**

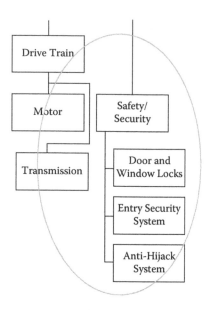

**Figure 8.14   Smaller deliverables.**

"Occasionally, you may find it difficult to define an activity for a particular deliverable because it may be unfamiliar. In this case, try to "break down" the deliverable into smaller deliverables (another level; Figure 8.14). Continue the breakdown process until a smaller deliverables becomes familiar. Then try to define new activities for the "finer" deliverables.

"In the example in Figure 8.14, further breakdown of "Safety/Security" produced deliverables that are now familiar — "Door and Window Locks," etc.

"If further breakdown does not work, try working through your difficulty with another team member — maybe a subject matter expert (SME).

"As you are planning your deliverables and activities, you might "surface" difficulties you cannot resolve at that moment. To manage these difficulties, we will be using the "parking lot" concept. I will be posting a flipchart with the title of "Parking Lot." When you encounter a difficulty you cannot resolve immediately, bring it to me. We will record the item and list you as the person highlighting it. Then after the Session, we will have more time available to resolve it. There also will be difficulties you can resolve, but only with a stated assumption — a statement

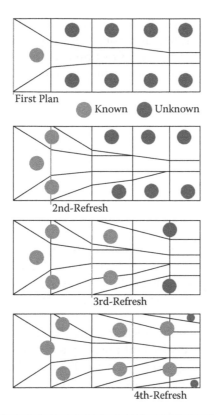

**Figure 8.15 The "folded map."**

considered *true* until proven otherwise. As with difficulties, bring to me your assumptions and we will record them as project assumptions.

"Before you begin, we need to discuss another item: how much should we plan? The projected timeline for our project is about XX months. It is unrealistic during this planning session for me to assume that you will know all your activities for the entire project. The concept involved here is the "window of knowledge" and that the window "moves" through time.

"Figure 8.15 shows the concept of the "folded map." It gives a preview of how we will manage our time-limited but periodic refreshes. Periodic "refreshes" will help us keep our plan up-to-date and provide the necessary data to manage our project.

"I want you to concentrate on your deliverables and their activities for the first X months. In addition, define any activities you have knowledge of beyond the X months and to the project endpoint.

"You have your supplies and instructions, and it is time to establish your activities. Please be as neat as possible. This step is time boxed — you have (xxx minutes). At the end of that time, we will assess our progress and extend the time as necessary. I am here to help you in any manner. If you have any questions, get with me.

"Otherwise let's go to work!"

That said, pass out the 3 × 5-inch Post-Its and other supplies and facilitate the session as necessary.

## Hints

There can be times when either you have not completed the PBS build-down or your team does not like what you have built. When this occurs, you can recover by deploying the planning team to build down the PBS. Just think of this as a pre-step for Step 4. When this occurs, buy-in will happen naturally: if they build it, they will like it and you will have your buy-in.

Keep the activities as Post-Its. There frequently is a team member with a PC and project management software. He or she may try to get you to abandon the Post-Its in favor of the PC. This may seem reasonable, but using PC software at this point will always be detrimental to your team effort. The issue is: what does your entire team do while that one person is entering the activity data? They will be doing nothing and you will soon "lose them." Stay with the Post-Its!

This step is half finished before it starts. An activity consists of a verb and a noun. The noun comes from the PBS — available at the beginning of Step 4. The only tasks left for Step 4 are to decide on the proper verbs and write out the Post-Its. Neither task requires a great deal of time. Try to keep your time box short — set a high work pace.

If an individual is having extreme difficulty establishing his or her activities, you may need to step in and help. Do not hesitate to deploy an SME with the individual if you cannot help. The action itself (i.e., assigning an SME) often can motivate the individual's thought process.

Frequently, there is another issue: how many people should be assigned to each activity? Some members will use this issue in defining their deliverables and activities. Try to delay this issue until Step 6 ("Assigning the Resources"). Suggest instead that the number of people assigned does not affect the activity definition; this is not always true but should help to delay the question until the time is right.

You may need to address the question of "how much should we plan?" If your project is lengthy and complicated, then your chance is low of planning the entire project in one session. In this case, you need to discuss with your team their "window of knowledge." The concept of the folded map will help you explain this issue. Settle this issue by team consensus; but if consensus is lacking, you will have to decide. Luckily, you can delay this issue until you have completed the first pass of the Process. At that time, you and your team will know a lot more about your team's "window of knowledge."

There should be one activity to start the project and one activity to finish it. These activities should be coving the topmost project deliverable. These activities are the "Start" and the "Finish" activities.

## Chapter 9

# Step 5
# Building the Physical Logical Diagram (The Network)

## Background

In this step, your team will be building the physical logical diagram, subsequently referred to as "the Network." Every process has a "quality step," a step establishing the quality of the overall process. Step 5 is the Process's quality step; take the time to perform this step as completely as possible. The resulting Network logic (order of activities to each other) is the basis for the project's schedule. If there are flaws in the logic, there will flaws in the schedule.

### The Network Is a Time-Oriented Diagram

The PBS (product breakdown structure) was organized as the project is assembled — an assembly diagram. The Network is a time-oriented diagram, organized by the logical order of activities (Figure 9.1).

We normally speak of it as organized "left-to-right." The starting Post-It is labeled "S" and the finishing Post-It is labeled "F." This step usually is the most interesting to your planning team. It is an extremely valuable step for many reasons. It is really just a big puzzle and your planning team knows how it all fits together.

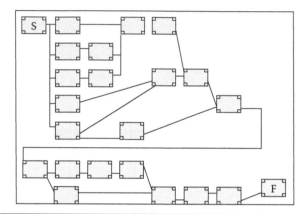

**Figure 9.1 The logical order of activities.**

## The Most Common Network Flaw

One of the most common network flaws is to establish the logic while assuming *limited resources*. Most team members will build the logic of their activities with this assumption — they assume that *they* are the limited resources! This is very natural and you will need to place special emphasis on an assumption that is just the opposite — *they* are indispensable. As they build their network's logic, they need to assume *unlimited resources*. The issue of how *resources* affect the project will be resolved during scheduling.

# JIT Training

Since the beginning of modern project management, three network styles have developed: (1) PERT (Program Evaluation Review Technique), (2) CPM (Critical Path Method), and (3) PDM (Precedence Diagramming Method).

## Program Evaluation Review Technique (PERT)

The Program Evaluation Review Technique (PERT) was the first network style identified with modern project management. It was developed in the early 1950s for a secret national defense project by the DoD (U.S. Department of Defense).

In PERT (Figure 9.2), the activities are contained in large circles and the arrows show their relationships. There is a single relationship possible: finish an activity and then start another. This relationship is a Finish-to-Start (F-S) relationship. The PERT style network has fallen in into disuse in favor of either the CPM or PDM.

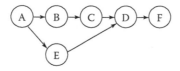

**Figure 9.2    Program Evaluation Review Technique (PERT).**

## Critical Path Method (CPM)

Most literature sources agree that Dupont (E.I.) de Nemours & Co developed the Critical Path Method (CPM) in the late 1950s (Figure 9.3). In CPM, the activities are located on the arrows (arcs) and the circles (nodes) are points of connection for the logic. Again, there is only the Finish-to-Start (F-S) relationship available. This orientation of activities represented by arrows is unique to CPM. This unique feature requires another form of arrow (arc) — "the dummy activity." A dummy activity allows for an exclusivity relationship between the converging paths of a network. Today, CPM is of historical interest and described (used) only in project management literature.

## Precedence Diagramming Method (PDM)

The Precedence Diagramming Method (PDM; Figure 9.4) is the third and the most modern style. An article from the University of Maryland in 1969 first described PDM. It became popular in the 1970s with the advent of the PC and project management software. The box represents an activity, and the arrow represents the relationship of the activities. The PDM style appears to be the same as PERT but there is a significant difference — PDM has four different relationship types:

1. Finish-to-Start (F-S; Figure 9.5). This relationship is the "normal relationship" and can cover 100 percent of a detailed project plan. It can define any real-life situation and therefore can be used exclusively. In Figure 9.5, interpret the F-S relationship as follows: you cannot start "Develop Specs" until "Define Reqts" is finished. The numbers to the left of the description constitute the unique identifier (UI).

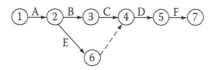

**Figure 9.3    Critical Path Method (CPM).**

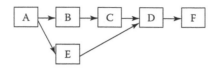

**Figure 9.4   Precedence Diagramming Method (DPM).**

2. Start-to-Start (S-S; Figure 9.6). This relationship is valuable to "lock" the start of one activity to the start of another. In Figure 9.6, you cannot start "Order Hardware" until you start "Moneys Released."
3. Finish-to-Finish (F-F; Figure 9.7). This relationship is valuable to "lock" the finish of one activity to the finish of another. The relationship in Figure 9.7 reads as activity 37 (Design Layout) can finish as soon as activity 65 (Publish Arch.) is finished.
4. Start-to-Finish (S-F; Figure 9.8). This relationship is infrequently used and not implemented in most PC software. The example in Figure 9.8 says that you cannot finish "Coding" until you have started "System Test."

These four different relationships are presented here to round out your education regarding PDM. In most projects, only the F-S relationship is used. Experience tells us that any use of the other three relationships is unnecessary and not desirable; the F-S relationship can describe all real-life situations.

## Lag

There is another feature of PDM not contained in the other network styles, and that is *lag* (Figure 9.9). A lag is a delay on the relationship between activities. In Figure 9.9, there is a ten-day lag (lag = 10) between the finish of "Define Reqts" and the start of "Develop Specs." This can be a valuable feature with some limitations. If the lag is truly a time delay, then its use is appropriate, such as "mailing time" or "deliver time." A delay consumes no resources and represents a situation beyond the project manager's control. Its use is inappropriate if it is intended to "hide" an activity. Because most PC software does not display the lag on network diagrams, it can be a confusion factor. Its use is only evident in the dates contained in the project schedule.

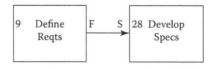

**Figure 9.5   A Finish-to-Start (F-S) relationship.**

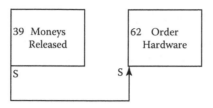

**Figure 9.6   A Start-to-Start (S-S) relationship.**

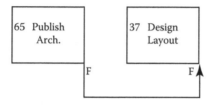

**Figure 9.7   A Finish-to-Finish (F-F) relationship.**

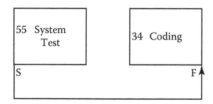

**Figure 9.8   A Start-to-Finish (S-F) relationship.**

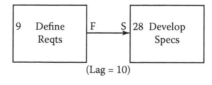

**Figure 9.9   The lag.**

## How the Network Goes Together

The Network is constructed of the activities — those now attached to their corresponding deliverable (on the PBS). The team members will remove their activities from the PBS and place them in logical order. As they place their activities, they should leave a ½-inch space between activities — that is, leave room for the arrows (relationships).

It is essential that the PBS remains intact, so remove only the 3 × 5-inch Post-Its.

## Where to Build the Network

Assemble the Network on another clean sheet of banner paper. If there is limited space on the walls, you can create space by dropping the PBS lower on the same wall and placing the new banner paper where the PBS once was. If using flipchart paper, you will need to overlap the sheets and tape their seams. Taping the seams will create a contiguous, portable sheet of paper similar to banner paper.

## Organize Sub-teams if Necessary

Large projects can have natural divisions of labor — separate types of deliverables and activities. If this is a fact for your project, you need to organize the development of the Network accordingly. Say, for example, there are four distinct areas of effort (food, entertainment, safety and security, and area maintenance) and you have 20 team members. Your team of 20 will find it difficult working on a single Network. You best divide the team into the four sub-teams. The sub-teams will lay out their networks and later combine their networks on to one project-level Network. There might be other ways of accomplishing the same end-result but experience tells us that this works with large planning teams. If the planning team is small (five or less), then a single network is possible.

Also, if you establish the Network via the sub-team concept, you will need to assign "blocks" of unique identifiers (UIs) for each sub-team; for example, "food" will use 100–199 as their unique identifiers, etc. Assigned blocks will prevent teams from using another team's unique identifiers.

## How to Get Started

As your team (or teams) begins this step, they may have trouble getting started. A simple starting technique is the placement of their "Start" and "Finish" activities — "Start" in the upper-left corner and "Finish" in the lower-right corner (Figure 9.10).

Generally, their next activities are related to organizing their sub-team activities: "Develop Possible Menus," "Research Food Vendors," "Review [local] Health

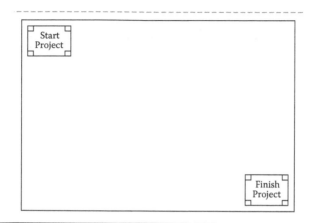

**Figure 9.10  "Start" and "Finish" activities.**

Standards," "Conduct Vendor Interviews," "Decide on Vendor," etc. (Figure 9.11). Note that the UIs have not been assigned.

When the team is satisfied with their activities' logical order, they draw arrows to define relationships. The next group placed is usually activities defining process deliverables, such as "Publish Menus," "Define Vendor Contracts," "Publish Storage Standards," "Publish Prep Standard," etc. (Figure 9.12).

Next, place activities that deliver lower-level deliverables, and so forth.

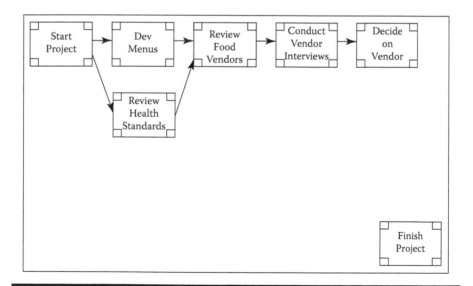

**Figure 9.11  Activities are related to organizing.**

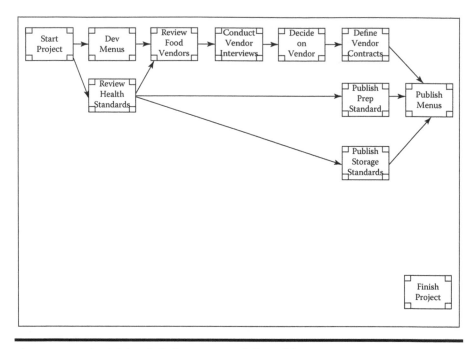

**Figure 9.12    Activities defining process deliverables.**

## *Ask the Right Question*

At any point in Step 5, your team's progress can slow to a stop. The problem might be: "What [Post-It] goes next?" The trick to re-starting the team is to teach them to ask the right question. The question (what is next) is: "What activity can start as soon as this one is finished?" An activity preceding another is a predecessor (activity). This questioning process becomes (1) take an activity (from the PBS), (2) find its predecessor, and (3) place the activity (the one in hand) to the right side of its predecessor, leaving a ½-inch gap. The Network is assembled in this manner. This implies that the only relationship you will use is a "Finish-to-Start" — most probably the case. There will be occasions where one of the other relationship types might be best and you will recognize when it is necessary.

## *Parallel Paths*

Another question often asked is: "How can I define parallel activities (parallel paths)?" There is a simple answer: "You do not define parallel paths because the network's logic does it for you." Here is the reasoning; if two activities require the same predecessor and, in turn, both are predecessors to another activity, then the two activities in question are "on parallel paths." In this manner, parallel paths are built naturally by asking and answering the question: "What goes next?"

## Interconnect the Sub-team Networks

Once the sub-teams have established their individual networks, they need to find if there is any connectivity with other sub-teams (their networks). This process is highly dependent on the number of sub-teams and their level of completion. All sub-teams must be reasonably complete with their network before the connectivity process can begin. If this process starts too soon, difficulties between the teams can develop. Experience tells us that sub-teams will have little patience with interruptions (by other teams) until they have completed their own networks. You can either sense when the time is right or ask whether all the sub-teams are ready to proceed.

The connective "device" is the activities' unique identifiers (UIs). The sub-teams are connecting with other sub-teams (networks) through the UIs. As they find predecessors for their activities on other sub-team's networks, they record this relationship on their activities (Post-Its).

## Now Combine It All

Once separate networks are complete, combine them on one chart — the project-level Network. There is a trick here also. You must begin the project-level Network with a "project timeline" (Figure 9.13). Start the timeline with your "Start" activity — placed in the middle of the left side of the chart. Then place any activities delivering major milestones to the right of "Start" and in the order they need to occur. The project timeline is complete with the "Finish" activity. The timeline provides the basis for combining the sub-teams' networks on the project-level Network.

To "link" a sub-team network to the project-level Network, they need to find an activity that starts their network. A start could either be an activity on the timeline ("a starting connection") or it could be another sub-teams' activity. This additional predecessor is added to their activity as a predecessor — on the Post-It (Figure 9.14).

In this example (Figure 9.14), activity "123" has two predecessors: "345" from their own network and "599" from the timeline. In this manner, the timeline is the "link" between the sub-teams (network) and the project-level Network (Figure 9.15).

This combining step can be confusing, so proceed slowing and methodically with the help of the entire team. Approach the combining process by asking one

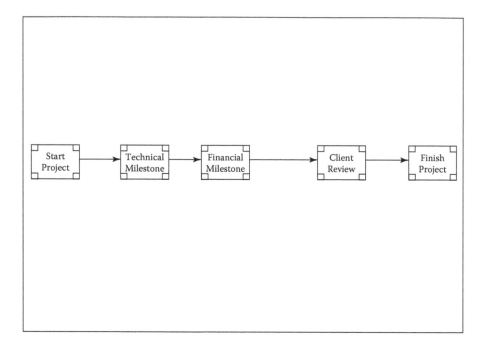

**Figure 9.13  The timeline.**

sub-team at a time to move their network to the project-level Network chart. This sub-team makes their "starting" connection to the timeline and waits for the other sub-teams to move their networks. Once all sub-teams have connected to the timeline, then they can connect (if any) to each other's networks. The combining process finishes when each sub-team's "finishing activity" connects either to another network or to any activity on the timeline or to the "Finish Project" activity on the timeline.

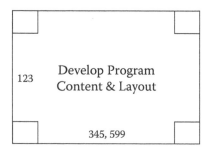

**Figure 9.14  Additional predecessor added.**

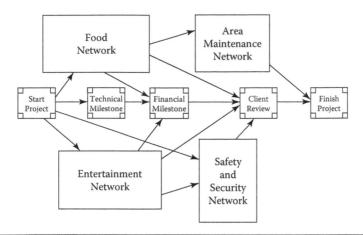

**Figure 9.15   The project-level Network.**

## *How to Draw Arrows*

There is a convention regarding how to draw arrows (relationships). And it is simple; the left side of a Post-It (now an activity) represents the "start" — the only *entry point* to an activity. The right side of a Post-It represents the "finish" — the only *exit point* from an activity. (See Figure 9.16.)

The top and bottom of the Post-It are simply "off-limits" as either the start or the end of an arrow. As teams draw their arrows, they have a tendency to be sloppy about where the arrow begins and ends. You will need to instruct them regarding this convention and follow up to see that they maintain it.

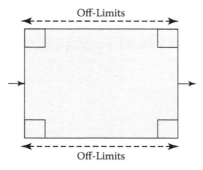

**Figure 9.16   The top and bottom of the Post-It.**

### Keep the PBS Current

During this step, it is very common to find that "something is missing." If an activity is missing, then a deliverable is missing and it should be added to the PBS. You need to keep this idea always in front of your team. Make sure they take the time to add the deliverable (on the PBS) and develop an activity to deliver that deliverable. It is essential to maintain the PBS as a current, useable, and living document throughout the entire project.

## Let's Practice

In Step 4 we develop the activities and place them over the corresponding deliverables (Figure 9.17).

Since we are a small team, we decide to all work on the same network. We build a work area on the wall with flipchart paper and masking tape. We had forgotten the "Start" and "Finish" activities, so we write them out, and place them in the new work area to begin our network (Figure 9.18).

Next, we place those activities that "organize" a project — that is, kickoff meeting, planning session, budget (money), and schedules (timing). Then we place the activities that produce the "process deliverables" (Figure 9.20). The process deliverables (as activities) form a column because they can all begin at the same time and we have assumed "unlimited resources."

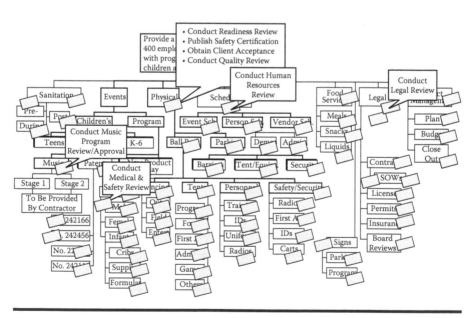

**Figure 9.17    Place Post-Its® over deliverables.**

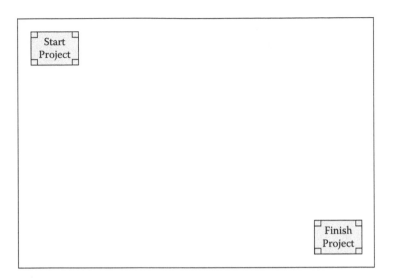

**Figure 9.18  Begin our network.**

Then the "big bang" occurs: all legs of the deliverables (now as activities) begin. However, it becomes obvious that we would quickly run out of room on the work area, so we decide to rearrange the network (Figure 9.21). Now with this new organization, we can expand the network with a series of paths representing the four major areas of effort (Figure 9.22).

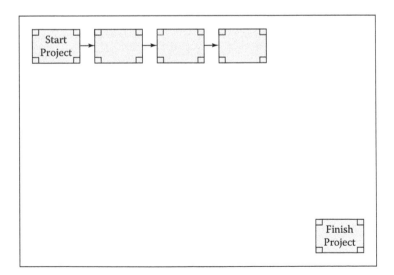

**Figure 9.19  Activities that "organize."**

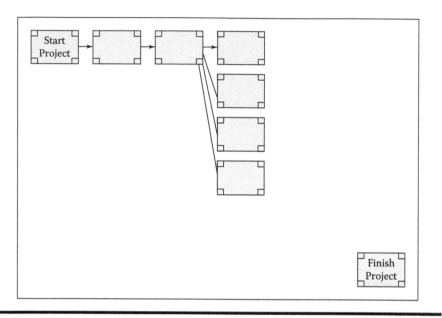

**Figure 9.20    Process deliverables.**

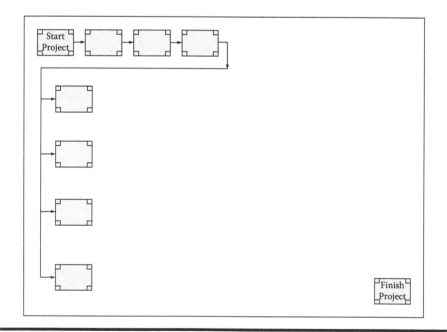

**Figure 9.21    Rearrange the network.**

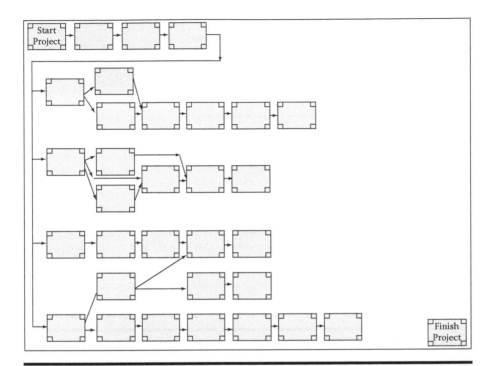

**Figure 9.22   A series of paths.**

We continue with higher-level activities and identify assembly point activities (Figure 9.23). We are now essentially complete with these last additions but we decide to include some post-event activities (Figure 9.24).

We then "step back" from the project-level Network and discover that something is missing. We add an extra lag of deliverables to the PBS and the corresponding extra activities (marked "E" in Figure 9.25) to the Network. This completes Step 5. We finish the day by identifying risks — 35 risk events are identified by brainstorming for only five minutes. We stop and decide to "pick up" the effort again the next day.

## Specific Facilitation Instructions

This facilitation instruction addresses two different facilitation situations caused by whether (1) you have subdivided your team or (2) you have kept the team together.

(Optional — if organized by sub-teams):

Because we are organized by sub-teams, this step will have two parts: Part 1 involves developing your

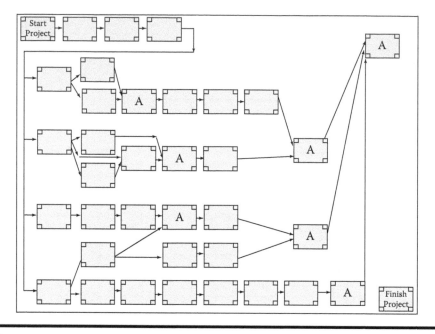

**Figure 9.23   Assembly point activities.**

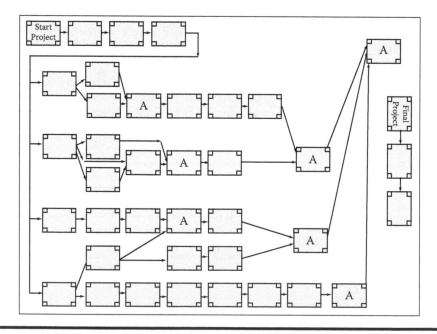

**Figure 9.24   Post-event activities.**

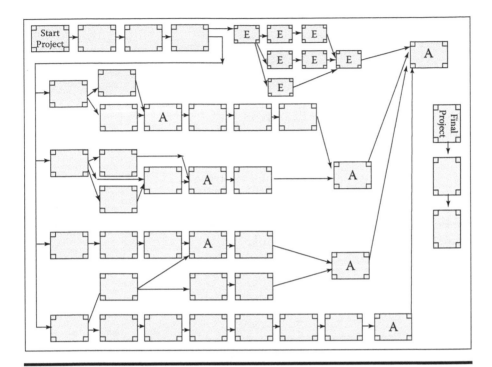

**Figure 9.25   Extra activities (marked "E").**

sub-team activities into your own network, and Part 2 involves combining the sub-team networks on a project-level Network (Figure 9.26). I will give you instructions for the combining part later.

Now we are ready to build the Network. As a reminder, the PBS was deliverable oriented, an assembly diagram. The Network is a logical order of your activities — assembled timewise (left-to-right). First, we need to create another working surface (chart) on the wall. If sufficient wall space is not available, move the PBS down on the same wall. Then assemble a new, blank chart on this newly available space. If we are using flip-chart paper, overlap the papers and tape the entire seam — this makes the chart portable.

Now move just your activities off the PBS and to the blank chart. Make sure to leave behind the deliverables (3 × 3 Post-Its). As you move your activities, place your starting activity on the left side of the chart and your finish activity on the right side of the chart (Figure 9.27).

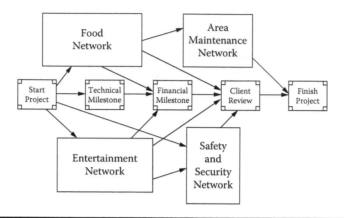

**Figure 9.26  The Project-Level Network.**

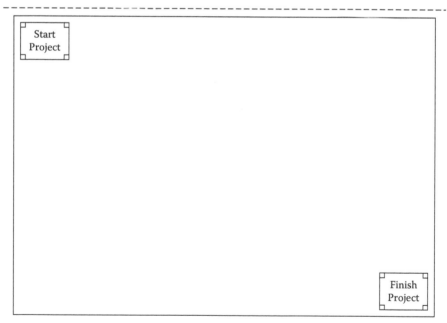

Activities are Related to Organizing

**Figure 9.27  Activities are related to organizing.**

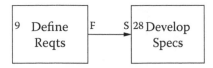

**Figure 9.28   The Finish-to-Start relationship.**

As you develop your network, arrange activities in the order that they should occur (timewise). After you find and place your starting activity, you will find and attach all activities that require the starting activity as a predecessor. In this manner, you are asking what activity must be finished before this activity can begin. This relationship is a "Finish-to-Start (F-S)" relationship (Figure 9.28).

After you have moved over your activities, they may seem scattered and unorganized (Figure 9.29). I hope you can remember their order and your reasons for their order. If you find you are having difficulty remembering their order, draw arrows between them *as you*

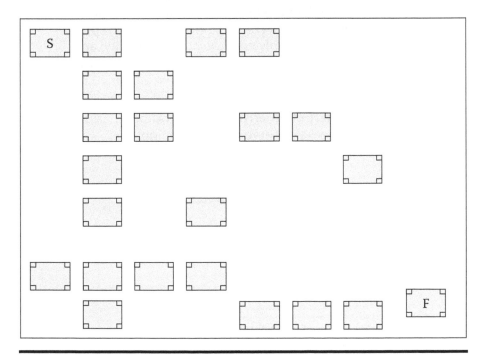

**Figure 9.29   Scattered and unorganized.**

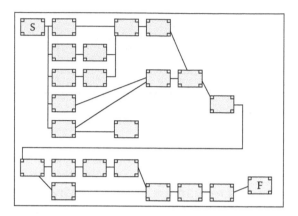

**Figure 9.30  Draw your arrows.**

*place them.* Otherwise, wait to draw your arrows until after you have assembled them and you are satisfied with their order (Figure 9.30).

Let me say something about drawing your arrows. There is a convention related to how to draw arrows (relationships). It is quite simple. The left side of a Post-It represents the 'start'— the only *entry point* to an activity; and the right side of a Post-It represents the 'finish' — the only *exit point* from an activity.

The top and bottom of the Post-It are 'off-limits,' either as the start of an arrow or the end of an arrow (Figure 9.31). Please observe this convention.

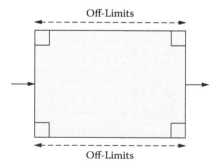

**Figure 9.31  The top and bottom of the Post-It.**

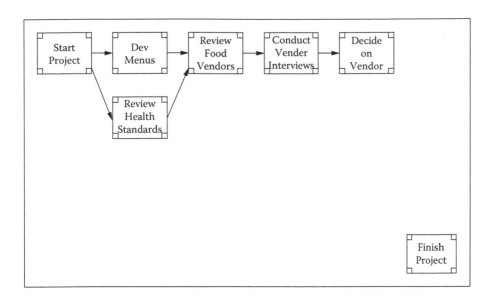

**Figure 9.32  Activities are related to organizing.**

It is essential that your network represent the correct order (logic) of the activities. If the logic of the network is wrong, all calculations and schedules will be wrong.

One assumption that you need to base your logic on is that *you have unlimited resources*. This assumption will allow you to connect your activities as they 'could be done.' There will be ample time later to consider the effect of resource limitations on the project.

After the Network's starting activity, it is normal for multiple activities to start at the same time — causing a column of activities. This column of activities usually comprises those activities that organize the project (Figure 9.32).

The next group of activities consists of those providing process deliverables. Then place the activities covering the lower-level deliverables.

Usually, the legs of the PBS produce a pattern of paths through the Network. The last group of activities consists of those associated with the topmost deliverable. Mixed in between these groups are the project management activities and those activities called 'assembly point activities.'

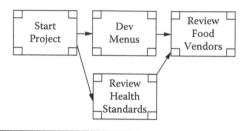

**Figure 9.33  Parallel paths.**

Do not concern yourself with how to define parallel paths (of activities). The question-and-answer process will establish the order of the activities and will naturally define when there are parallel paths. Listen to the definition of a parallel path: if two activities call for the same predecessor and both are called for as a predecessor to another activity, then the two activities are in parallel paths.

Figure 9.33 shows parallel paths; 'Dev Menus' and 'Review Health Standards' are on parallel paths because both call for 'Start Project' as a predecessor and both are called for as a predecessor for 'Review Food Vendors.'

During this step, it is very common to find that 'something is missing.' If an activity is missing, it means a deliverable is missing and needs to be added to the PBS. Take the time now to add the deliverable (on the PBS) and develop an activity to deliver that deliverable. In this manner, we will keep the PBS current and make it a useful, living document.

After you have drawn your relationships (as arrows), record on each activity its predecessor(s). Add this information on the Post-Its on the bottom edge and between the corner boxes. In the example in Figure 9.34, the activity '123' has activity '345' as its predecessor. In this way, you have captured your network's logic as predecessors in a written format. This format will be useful later as input format for PC software data entry.

Before you begin, there are several important instructions:

1. Please be neat as possible.
2. Order your activities as if you have infinite resources.

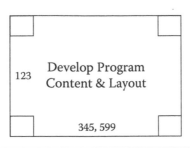

**Figure 9.34   Additional predecessor added.**

3. Leave space between activities and draw in the arrows (relationships).
4. If you find you are missing activities, go back to Step 3 and define the deliverables, etc.
5. Label any new activity with one of your unique identifiers.
6. Write each activity's predecessor on the Post-Its.

This step is time boxed for XX minutes. We will review your progress at the end of the period and extend the time as necessary. If you have any questions, please let me know.

The supplies are here so, let's go to work!"

(Optional — if organized by sub-teams):

Part Two: now it is time to combine all the sub-team networks into a single, project-level Network. As you can see, I have laid out a large chart to help us combine all our networks. And I have ordered the project timeline down the middle as a reference for your networks (Figure 9.35).

Before we can combine the networks, we need to find any connections you have to (1) another sub-team's network and (2) the project timeline. It is time for you to make these connections by reviewing your activities' 'outside predecessors.' Again, the question is: what activities (outside my own) need to finish before I can start this activity? As you find your predecessors, write them with your own network's predecessors on the Post-Its (Figure 9.36).

In this diagram, activity '123' now has an added predecessor ('599') — from the project timeline. The "comma" between the predecessors is a delimiter.

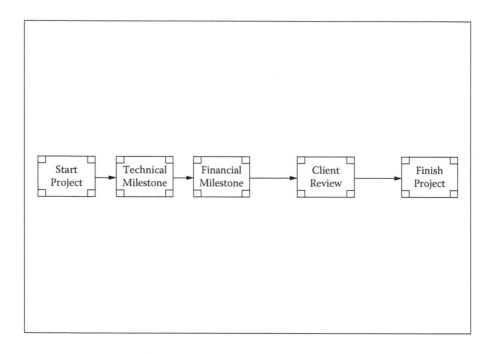

**Figure 9.35   The timeline.**

It will be essential that you connect your network's start-ing activity either to the project timeline or to another network. All sub-teams' networks must have only one 'finish activity.' If there is no natural 'finishing activity,' then create a milestone activity to bring all your activities together. This milestone then represents the delivery of

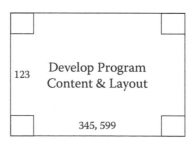

**Figure 9.36   Additional predecessor added.**

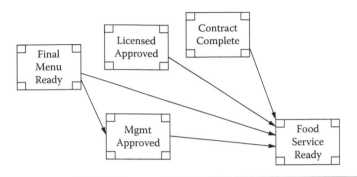

**Figure 9.37   Create a milestone activity.**

that portion of the larger project, for example, 'Food Service Ready' (Figure 9.37).

It is very possible that you can have multiple 'starting activities' but all activities except the 'Finish Project' activity must have another activity calling for it as its predecessor — only one activity is the ending activity. A simple rule: if you find an activity not called for as a predecessor to another activity, then either something is missing (find it, define it, and place it) or it is a 'finishing activity.' A finishing activity is usually the last activity in a path. In this case, connect this last activity to your (sub-team) network's last activity, as above. There is one other possibility — this activity is not needed! Occasionally, you may find an activity that even though it occurred in earlier projects, it is unnecessary here.

You will have another XX minutes to find the connections (logic) to and from your network.

Now it is time to combine the individual networks. As I call you, move your network (reason for portability) onto the project-level Network and link them together (Figure 9.38).

This combining step can be confusing, so we will proceed slowly and methodically as one team. I will lead and ask each sub-team (one at a time) to move its network to the Network chart. If the sub-team has a "starting" connection to the timeline, they draw that connection (arrow) and wait for the other sub-teams to move their networks. Once all sub-teams have connected to the

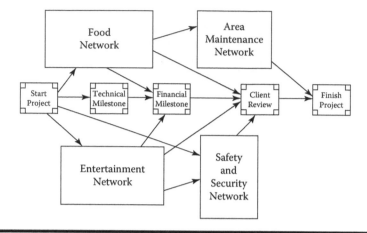

**Figure 9.38   The project-level Network.**

timeline, then they can connect to each other's network as guided by the predecessors they found earlier. We will finish when each sub-team's "finishing activity" is connected either to another network, to the timeline, or to the 'Finish Project' activity. It is essential that all activities connect to other activities — there can be only one last activity, 'Project Finish.'

This second part is time boxed for XX minutes.

We will review your progress at the end of the period and extend the time as necessary. If you have any questions, please let me know.

Let's go to work!"

# Hints
## The Quality Step

Step 5 is the quality step for the Process. Let this step proceed until you and your team are satisfied with the resulting Network.

## Do Not Let It Drag Out

On the other hand, do not let this step "drag on" too long. There will be at least one more opportunity to refine the Network — the Second Pass (Steps 3 through 8).

You must constantly assess your team's energy and attention span (interest). When there seems to be a lull in effort, maybe it is time for a break.

## Another Value

If you have a mixed team, experience-wise, you will find this step extremely valuable. The amount of knowledge transfer from the "experienced" to "novice" is phenomenal. The fact that your team is working with a visual format of activities enhances this transfer and aids in information retention. The Process is not promoted as a team-building exercise, but the personal interaction that occurs makes it very clearly a "teamwork enhancement process." When the Network is complete, everyone will know what is expected of him or her and what everyone else is doing — they are all interconnected.

## Your Facilitation

Your main job during this step is facilitation — anything you need to do to keep it "moving." However, you also must prepare your project management activities. Prepare them as a sub-team network with the same rules and actions — set an example. Your activities (and deliverables) are essential to the management of the team but need not appear on the project-level Network at this time; add them later when you take your project to the PC software.

## Do Not Get into Details

Most project managers also are capable technologists in some manner. Whenever presented with an uncomfortable situation, it is human nature to fall back to an area of competency. As the Session facilitator, you must not get too far into the details (area of competency). You need to stay above the details and let your team members manage them. If, however, you observe a sub-team having difficulties, you have to inquire as to the reason. Quickly determine the problem. If it is a problem with the Process, then you must dig into it. If it is a matter of technology, let the team members handle it. If they still cannot handle it, "park it" as an issue — and then move on.

## Not Needed

*Truly, there are times when deliverables and their activities are defined and not needed. Experience tells us that this is rare; but if they are identified at all, it is usually during Step 5.*

# Chapter 10

## Step 6
## Assigning the Resources

### Background

Your Network is now in place and ready to receive additional information. During Step 6, your team will identify each activity's resources information. To your team, this may seem a simple, unnecessary step. However, it is a psychological step — to "tie" an activity to a person. The value of this tie-in will become clearer in Step 7 (estimate the durations).

Resource information will be necessary when you perform resource allocation, i.e., arranging the activities' schedules to account for limited resources. PC software is perhaps best for resource allocation of complicated networks (i.e., more than 50 activities). However, in Part Three, you will be guided through resource allocation in a manual mode.

The duration of this step need not be very long. Experience tells us that 20 minutes should be long enough.

### JIT Training
#### Who Defines the Resources?

Frequently, when you call for the planning session, you will find those responding are not necessarily those individuals who will ultimately be working on the project. Hopefully, these individuals will know what is needed and how it all comes

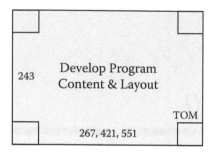

**Figure 10.1 Where do the resources go?**

together. Most of the time, they are subject matter experts (SMEs) but other times they are just simply someone who is available. In either case, you will have to "make the best of it." This fact of project life creates two broad categories of individuals involved in the definition process: (1) those who will work on the project and (2) SMEs.

## Where Do the Resources Go?

The resource information is entered on the rightmost edge of each Post-It and between the reserved boxes (Figure 10.1). In this figure, a specific individual ("TOM") has been identified to perform this activity.

If an SME is defining the resource, he or she will write in a "skill type" (Figure 10.2). Here, a skill type, "Project Manager," identifies the resource. Project teams can use short forms of identification, such as a person's initials, team member numbers, special codes, etc. If they use a code, they need to explain it to you.

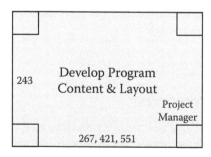

**Figure 10.2 A "skill type."**

### *Keep Track of Any Codes*

It will be important to develop and use a standard set of resource "codes." If you are using PC software, it is important to write the code exactly — the same each time. If the skill code is "cook's helper," do not use "Cook's Helper." This would define a different code — codes are case sensitive.

## Let's Practice

It is the next day. We have set aside three hours to complete the Process. The project-level Network is complete and shows more than enough detail. The consensus is that we had more detail than needed. The team is experienced and three of the four members were actively involved in the planning and execution of last year's event. This level of experience causes us to view the PBS (product breakdown structure) from another point of view (Figure 10.3).

We decide that most of the lower-level deliverables (those shown in Figure 10.3 with "X"s through them) would remain on the PBS but not "made into" activities. Instead, these lower-level deliverables will become checklists — one list for each team member to follow and complete. The remaining deliverables make up the Network (Figure 10.4).

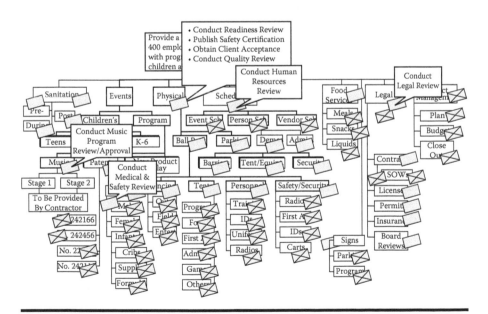

**Figure 10.3   The PBS from another point of view.**

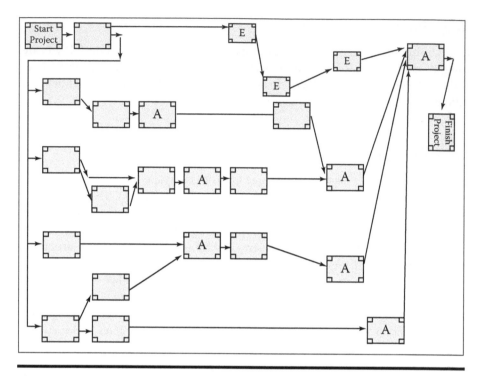

**Figure 10.4  The remaining deliverables.**

The team assigns either the resources' names or types (shown on the right edge; Figure 10.5). In 15 minutes, this step was completed.

## Specific Facilitation Instructions

"Now we need to identify the resource performing the activities. Some of you are assigned to the project and others of you are here to help plan the project. We are now going to assign to each activity, that activity's resource. If an activity is yours, write in your name. If you are here helping, write in the 'skill type.'

"Write the resource on the rightmost side and between the reserved boxes of the Post-Its®. If the project is your assignment, write in your name (Figure 10.6). In this figure, 'TOM' is the resource.

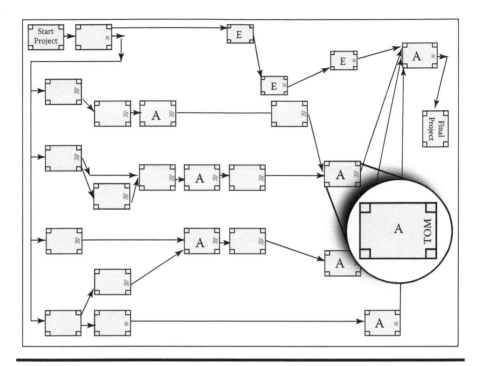

**Figure 10.5    The team assigns resources.**

"If you are helping, write in the skill type (Figure 10.7). Here, the skill type is 'Project Manager.' If you use any type of code, abbreviation, etc., then please show and define them for me.

"As we are defining resource codes, it will be important to have a standard set of any codes and to use them in an exacting manner. If the skill code is 'cook's helper' and you spelled it 'Cook's Helper,' it will be a different code — it is 'case sensitive.'"

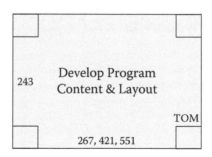

**Figure 10.6    Write in your name.**

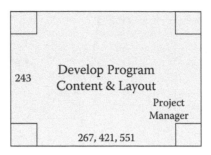

**Figure 10.7   Write in your skill type.**

As you define a code for a resource, please show it to me. I will enter it into a standard list of codes with their exact spelling.

"This step is time boxed for XX minutes. If you have any questions, please let me know.

"Otherwise, let's go to work."

## Hints
### Appears Simple

This step will appear very simple to your team. It is simple to perform but it does have an important impact on the project schedule. It also prepares the team for Step 7 — defining their durations. The combination of resources and durations will establish the other half of delegation — accountability. It is important that this step occur before Step 7.

## Later, Combine Steps

As your teams become more experienced with the Process, you could consider combining Steps 6 and 7 — and with experience, it is a natural combination.

# Chapter 11

# Step 7
# *Estimate the Durations*

## Background

It is now time for each team member to establish the timing parameter for their activities — their durations. The combination of a correctly defined network and the durations will establish the project's schedule.

### *Questions and Doubts*

It is common during this step to "surface" a large number of questions and doubts:

- How can I estimate something I have never done?
- How do I account for multiple resources in an activity?
- How do I know if the project and my activity will not occur at the same time as another project I have committed to?
- How can I estimate for an activity when I have little knowledge of future work factors (hours per day, numbers of simultaneous project, etc.)?
- How will I know if other team members will produce the deliverable I need to start mine?
- And many other questions, yet to be experienced.

All these questions are valid and answered by, "it's estimating." Estimating is, in fact, an educated guess regarding a not fully definable, future event. An estimate is just a guess and nothing more. If you are dealing with experienced team members, they may be reluctant (to provide a duration) because of a past bad experience — that is, they "got burned." All too often, an estimate "becomes a fact" — chiseled in stone. Somehow, you will have to break through their reluctance.

There are two methods built into the Process that will help. The first is the "second pass," and this is a good time to introduce this concept. A second pass means that after you have completed the entire Process, you will lead the team again back to Step 3 (Deliverables — PBS) and then through the remaining steps. The significance to your team members is that their duration estimates will be reviewed a second time, and they will have an opportunity to modify them, as they see fit.

The second method is the concept of assumptions. Throughout the Process, you need to emphasize the gathering, recording, and defining of assumptions. An assumption is a statement treated as a fact until it is proven true or false. You cannot let the lack of "hard and fast answers" slow your team's progress. When a difficulty arises that you cannot solve immediately, treat it with either a parking lot item or an assumption, and move on.

Team members also "throw up" questions for their own unknown reasons — some are not even related to the project. It is truly amazing to work with a team member all the way through to Step 7 and, all of a sudden, they become reluctant to provide an estimate — they are "stiff-arming you." Experience tells us that there are several approaches to handle a "stiff arm" and JIT training will demonstrate several (approaches).

## JIT Training

### *Handling a "Stiff Arm"*

Estimating blocks are common when experienced team members have had "esti-mates" turned into a fixed target or price. Such an event can turn even a rational person into an irrational estimator. When this is evident, a first approach is to remind them there will be several more steps during the Session when they can adjust their estimates. If they are still reluctant, then appeal to their understanding of the Process; you need durations to calculate the critical path and validate the project's target end-point. If still not moved, then explain that *you* will estimate their duration for them. Then set what you would consider a very high number — say, 100 days. Experience tells us (about 50 percent) that *your* high number will force an instant response, such as "No, no, not that much." Then state a very low number — say, one day. Again, you will receive an instant response, such as "No. No. Not that low." Now you know that their activity's duration range is between one and a hundred days! You can now remind them that you will probably use the high number for calculating the schedule, and their activity will certainly end up on the critical path. When this happens, you will be back again to "discuss" this same issue.

## *The Critical Path*

The concept of critical path is discussed in full detail during Step 8 (validating the project's timeline) but you will need an understanding during this step. In simplest terms, critical path is the path of activities whose total duration is the longest, time-wise, through the project.

## *No Estimate? There Can Be Reasons*

There are occasions when making an estimate is difficult, if not impossible. If a deliverable is very unfamiliar to a person, then there is no basis for estimating. Remember the concept of deliverables at the fourth level. If an estimate is not forthcoming at the fourth level, then maybe it can be made at the fifth or sixth level. This requires decomposition of the deliverable into finer and smaller deliverables. Frequently, a lower-level deliverable will "trigger" a familiarity (experience) not available at the higher-level deliverable. The aid of an SME can facilitate the decomposition process. If decomposition occurs, do not forget to update the PBS with this additional deliverable.

## *A PERT Estimate*

There is also the situation where the individual is honestly trying to estimate the duration but he or she is not making progress. This might be the time to introduce an estimating technique developed to handle situations dealing with unknowns. The technique is called a PERT estimate –(Program Evaluation Review Technique). The PERT technique was developed during the first computerized project management effort — the Polaris project. PERT estimates help when there is uncertainty in the activity. PERT is simply a weighted average. This method requires three estimates for the activity: (1) the most likely (ML), (2) the optimistic (OP), and (3) the pessimistic (PS).

In the example in Figure 11.1, the individual has provided three estimates: ML = 10, OP = 6, and PS = 20. A PERT calculation would provide 11 days. If a single point estimate is used, it would be the same as the PERT "most likely" estimate and the activity's duration would be ten days. The large value of the pessimistic estimate (PS) increases the duration by one day. In a real-life situation, you would round up any remainder to the nearest whole number. A PERT estimate will provide some measure of contingency for activity unknowns.

$$\frac{OP + 4x(ML) + PS}{6}$$

Example:

OP = 6
ML = 10
PS = 20

$$\frac{6 + 4x(10) + 30}{6} = 11 \text{ days}$$

**Figure 11.1   The PERT is simply a weighted average.**

## Handling Multiple Resources

In a perfect world, assign only one individual to each activity. However, there will be activities requiring multiple resources. Your first preference should be to have only one person per activity. If an activity appears to require multiple resources, then you could request that the deliverable be decomposed to cause smaller deliverables and resulting smaller activities. Smaller activities generally require only one resource. It is not necessary to have only one resource per activity during the first pass. However, for the final project network, it will be best to have one resource per activity.

## Best Estimates but Not Their Tightest

You want your team's best estimates for their activities, but not their tightest (shortest). You need their estimates now but they will have many opportunities to change them later.

## Estimates in Days

The best unit of measure for duration is "days." The smallest activity duration would then be one day. Even one day may seem too long for simple activities. The fourth-level concept allows for activities of a reasonable size without too much detail. After Step 8, it is advisable to perform a second pass through the Process. During that pass, you will be applying some parameters regarding the maximum duration of special activities — those on the critical path. However, at this time, you simply need durations for each activity to enable Step 8.

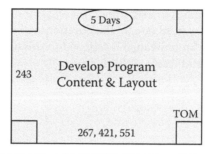

**Figure 11.2    The duration is calculated.**

## Where to Place the Duration

Write the durations on the Post-Its® at the very top and between the reserved boxes (Figure 11.2). Circle the durations to distinguish them from the unique identifiers. The circling of the duration will be important as your team performs critical path analysis. Experience tells us that teams can confuse the five-day duration with the activity's unique identifier ("243"). This mistake could make a big difference in the duration estimate for a project.

## Duration versus Workload

Some of your team members may be SMEs, and they are here to help you establish the project plan. They have already established the activities and built their network. Now it is time for them to estimate their durations. Because SMEs are not necessarily assigned to the project when they estimate the duration, they approach it from a different point of view. The SMEs' estimates are in workload — that is, number of hours. Their estimate should be for an average performer — not them. The activity's duration is calculated from the *workload* and an assumption regarding the *effective workday* (Figure 11.3). The effective workday is the number of hours per day an individual can work on the project.

Duration = Workload/Effective workday

Example:

Duration = 48 hrs/6 hrs per day = 8.0 days

**Figure 11.3    Duration from workload.**

In this example, the project's assumption for *effective workday* is six hours and the SME defined *workload* is 48 hours. The duration will then be eight days. It is important to note that as an individual is assigned to this activity, they will review the activity (deliverable) and reaffirm the duration.

## Let's Practice

We can start Step 7 as soon as the resources are assigned. There was no reluctance on the part of the team members to provide the necessary duration estimates. There is some difficulty in estimating durations for the subcontractor responses (deliverables) such as turn-around times for menus, specifications for fencing, tenting, electrical, and water resources — we use what we think will be average durations. The subcontractors will later validate the averages. Our network is now ready for critical path analysis (Figure 11.4).

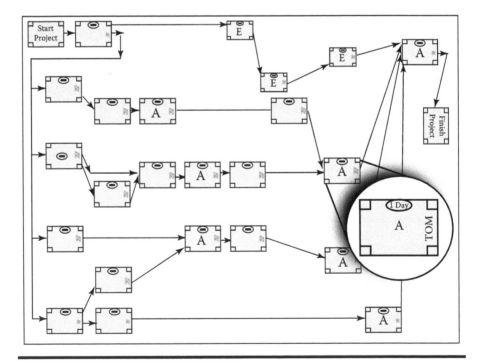

**Figure 11.4  Network is now ready for critical path analysis.**

## *Specific Facilitation Instructions*

During this step, you will estimate the durations of your activities. By duration, we mean the lapse time to perform an activity. Your duration estimates will be used to calculate the critical path for the project. The critical path is simply the longest, timewise, path through the Network. We will be estimating in days, so your smallest duration is a day. It is a day even if the activity takes only two minutes to perform. You are free to estimate what you think the activity's duration might be, and your estimates will be treated as *just* an estimate. There will be a later time when you must commit to your estimates but for now, they are just estimates.

First, let me remind you that we will (probably) be executing the Process a second time (second pass). This means we need your estimates for your activities now, but you will have opportunities later to modify them.

You should write your durations on the Post-Its in the middle of the top and between the reserved boxes (Figure 11.5).

As you enter your durations, circle them. This circle helps us distinguish the duration from the unique identifier. You can imagine the effect on the project duration if you used 243 (the UI) days rather than the intended five days' duration. I really want an estimate you can meet —a duration that you feel is right. I want neither your lowest nor your highest. At this time, just use your average duration.

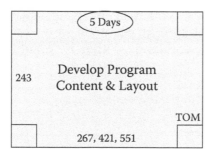

**Figure 11.5    The duration is posted.**

If you have difficulty estimating, you need to ask yourself why. If it is something you have never done, then redefine the deliverable and the activity. If it is something you have done but it was difficult, then add on a little extra duration.

If your activity has a wide range of possible durations, consider using the PERT equation. PERT is a technique for calculating the duration of an activity that has uncertainty. A PERT estimate requires three duration estimates: (1) most likely (ML), (2) optimistic (OP), and (3) pessimistic (PS).

$$\frac{OP + 4 \times (ML) + PS}{6}$$

Example:

OP = 6
ML = 10
PS = 20

$$\frac{6 + 4 \times (10) + 30}{6} = 11 \text{ days}$$

**Figure 11.6  The PERT is simply a weighted average.**

In this example in Figure 11.6, ML = 10, OP = 6, and PS = 20. The PERT calculation would result in a duration of 11 days. If you had used a single point estimate, it would be the same as the PERT "most likely" estimate — duration of ten days. The large value of the pessimistic estimate (20) increases the duration by one day. If your division leaves you a remainder, round up your duration to the nearest whole number.

Some of you are here to help us establish the project plan. You have already established the activities and built your network. Now as you estimate their durations, you will have to approach durations from a different point of view. Your estimates should be in workload — that is, number of hours.

Duration = Workload/Effective workday

Example:

Duration = 48 hrs/6 hrs per day = 8.0 days

**Figure 11.7  Duration from workload.**

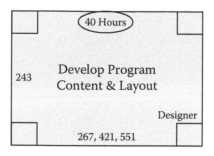

**Figure 11.8   Workload, in hours.**

This estimate should be for an average performer — not you. The duration is calculated from your *workload* estimate and the *effective workday*. The effective workday is the number of hours per day an individual can work on the project. The duration of your defined activities is calculated from their defined workload and an assumed effective workday (Figure 11.7).

In this example, the project's assumption for *effective workday* is six hours and your defined *workload* is 48 hours. The duration will then be eight days. This duration will be used in Step 8. As you enter your workload estimates on the Post-Its, indicate the workload in hours as indicated in Figure 11.8.

This step is time boxed for XX minutes. If you do not have any questions, let's get to work!"

# Hint

There will be situations where an individual still will refuse to provide an estimate. If it is obvious that they truly have no idea what the estimates should be, engage the help of an SME. This usually causes the individual to rethink his position and his estimate is forthcoming.

## Chapter 12

# Step 8
# *Verify the Project Timeline*

## Background

"Verifying the project timeline" is really nothing but performing network mathematics. Its prime purpose is to determine whether the project team can meet or exceed the targeted endpoint (timeline). In addition, while performing this step; the team acquires an understanding of how the critical path affects them and their individual activities. To the facilitator, an advantage of critical path analysis (CPA) is to keep the planning team fully engaged in the planning process. The mathematics of CPA are simple and can be performed without either a calculator or PC software. It completes the network mathematics set of PERT (Program Evaluation Review Technique). PC software can perform this step but for the sake of maintaining the planning team's interest, it is best performed *at this time* and *manually*. One of the "hidden" controversies in project management revolves around how CPA should be performed. There are three methods: (1) the all paths method, (2) the one method, and (3) the zero method. Interval mathematics is the basis for CPA, and the essential difference between the zero and one methods is how to manage the "interval."

## JIT Training

### *Three CPA Methods*

There are three different methods to perform CPA. They were all developed for different purposes. All three methods will arrive at the same endpoint date but will have different intermediate dates.

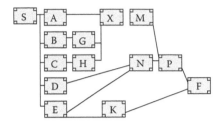

**Figure 12.1  All paths method.**

## *Dates versus Absolute Days*

When we speak of "dates," we are really referring to absolute periods. When performing CPA, we are dealing with whole numbers (1, 23, 51, etc,) representing your minimum period of lapse time — most frequently "days."

## *All Paths Method*

The all paths method is the simplest method and was developed to determine quickly the critical path. This method requires you to first identify all the different paths through the network.

In this example in Figure 12.1, there are six paths (S-A-X-M-P-F, S-B-G-X-M-P-F, S-C-H-X-M-P-F, S-D-N-P-F, S-E-N-P-F, S-E-K-F). Now add the duration along each path and the longest path is the critical path (Figure 12.2).

The S-B-G-X-M-P-F path's duration is 22 and it is the critical path. This example has only one critical path, but there can be one critical path, many critical paths, or even all paths can be critical. This method is very simple and easy to apply. Use it when you have a network of 50 or less activities with a few, simple paths and you are interested to know the critical path and the overall duration of your network.

## *The Zero Method*

The zero method is not a technically sound method but instead an expediency developed by authors and teachers to easily explain CPA. Its basis is zero — the

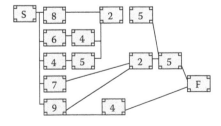

**Figure 12.2  Longest path is the critical path.**

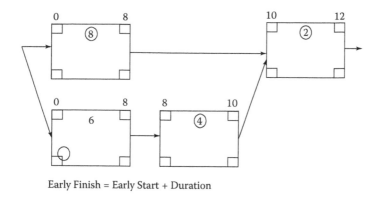

Early Finish = Early Start + Duration

**Figure 12.3   The zero method.**

first activity starts on the zero date (Figure 12.3). The numbers outside the activities are the "early dates." The number off the top left corner is the *early start* for the activity and the number off the top right corner is its *early finish*. The mathematics are simple: the *duration* plus the *early start* date is equal to the *early finish* date. The *early finish* date is then "carried" to the next activity (its early start).

The mathematics of the zero method is twice flawed. The first flaw begins with the use of zero as the early start date; there is no "zero" date in a calendar. The second flaw occurs when the early finish of an activity becomes the early start of a following activity. How can a following activity begin on the same date of its predecessor's early finished date? Perhaps you could see this flaw easier if this same example is scheduled (Figure 12.4). In this example, the activities on the bottom row point out the flaw in the zero method. The early start for the second activity is April 28 — after its predecessor is finished on the same date. The zero method ignores the concept of intervals. In case you were wondering, for scheduling purposes, all three methods ignore any non-work days.

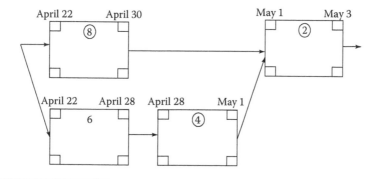

**Figure 12.4   Same example is scheduled.**

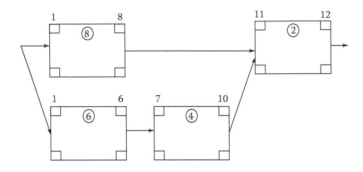

**Figure 12.5   The one method.**

## The One Method

The one method was developed for PERT, its mathematics were defined by a consulting company, and it was programmed by IBM. The one method's algorithm uses a "1" as the early start date for all activity that can begin immediately (Figure 12.5).

Only the one method will calculate the critical path correctly and allow for proper activity scheduling (Figure 12.6).

## Critical Path Analysis (CPA)

The one method will correctly calculate the critical path. The complete CPA process requires two passes through the network: the forward pass and the backward pass. The forward pass establishes the *earliest* each activity *can* start and finish, and the backward pass establishes the *latest* each activity *must* start and finish.

## Early Dates

The forward pass begins at the first activity and proceeds to the right — to the finishing activity. The resulting early dates (start and finish) are written off the upper

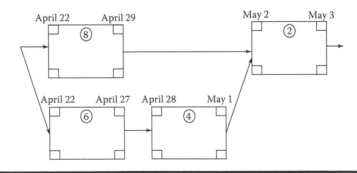

**Figure 12.6   Proper activity scheduling.**

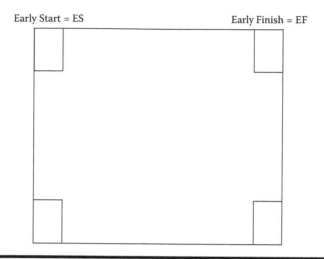

**Figure 12.7   Writing early dates off the upper corners.**

corners of the activity (Post-It) — to the left for early start and to the right for early finish (Figure 12.7).

## *Late Dates*

The backward pass begins at the last activity and proceeds to the left — to the starting activity. The resulting late dates (start and finish) are written off the bottom corners of the activity — to the left for late start and to the right for late finish (Figure 12.8).

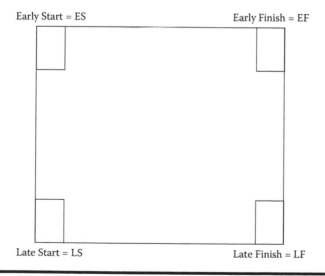

**Figure 12.8   Writing late dates off the bottom corners.**

The Post-Its'® corner boxes are reserved for schedule dates.

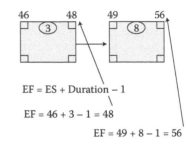

$$EF = ES + Duration - 1$$

$$EF = 46 + 3 - 1 = 48$$

$$EF = 49 + 8 - 1 = 56$$

**Figure 12.9   Forward pass.**

## Forward Pass

Begin the forward pass with "1." All activities starting immediately after the starting activity are given a "1" as their early start date. The activity's *early finish date* is the early start date *plus* the duration (of the activity) *minus* "1." The early finish date is then incremented by one and it now becomes the early start date for any following activity (Figure 12.9).

In the example in Figure 12.9, 46 plus 3 minus 1 equals the early finish date (48) for the first activity. This early finish date then is incremented by 1, and 49 becomes the early start date for the next activity. In turn, the second activity has an early finish date of 56 (49 + 8 − 1 = 56). Please note that this algorithm is for a finish-to-start relationship only. The "−1" accounts for the intervals. The increment of 1 between activities accounts for the fact that your workday interval is, say, 8:30 a.m. until 5:30 p.m.. PC software will allow for different workdays (interval).

An activity is called a sink if it calls for multiple predecessors' activities. In this special case, the latest, early finish is

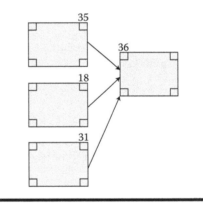

**Figure 12.10   The "sink" activity.**

incremented by one and it becomes the early start date for the sink activity. In the sink example in Figure 12.10, the latest early finish date of 35 becomes the early start date (35 + 1) for the sink activity. A more complicated diagram might help explain the forward and backward passes (Figure 12.11). The forward pass calculates the earliest the activities can start and finish and the latest early finish date of all ending activities becomes the early finish date (17) for the network (project).

## Backward Pass

The backward pass begins with the *early finish date* calculated by the forward pass. This early finish date is the earliest the entire project can be finished based on the logic of the network and the durations of the activities. The calculations for the backward pass are simply the reverse of the forward pass. When you added the duration for the

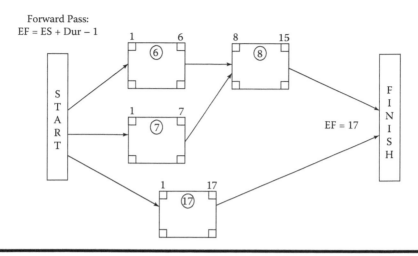

**Figure 12.11  A more complicated diagram.**

forward pass, you now subtract it. When you incremented by one for the forward pass, you now decrement by one. When you take the latest for many activities into a sink for the forward pass, you now take the earliest late start into a "source."

The example in Figure 12.12 shows a source — occurring during the backward pass. In this case, the earliest late start of "39" minus "1" becomes the late finish (39 − 1) of the source (activity 101). A source occurs when several activities call for a single activity as their predecessor.

The backward pass calculation for CPA uses this new set of algorithms (Figure 12.13). The early finish of 17 for the project becomes the late finish for the network and the late finish for the two last activities. When you subtract their durations and add back "1," their late starts are calculated (1 and 10) for the two paths. The top path now splits into two paths and their late finish is "9" — the late start of their following activity minus "1." In turn, their respective late starts are "4" and "3."

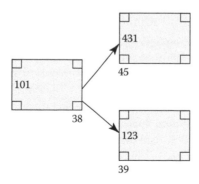

**Figure 12.12  A sink for the backward pass.**

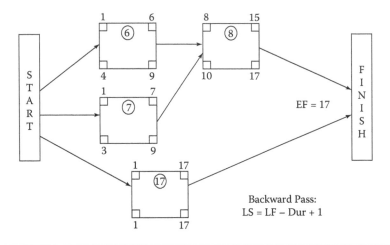

**Figure 12.13   The backward pass calculation.**

The backward pass has now established the latest that each activity can start and finish. Both CPA passes provide the basis for an additional CPA calculation — float. In turn, float is the basis for resources allocation.

## *Float*

The definition of "float" is the amount of time you can delay the start of an activity before you delay the project. The calculation of float is part of the mathematics of CPA. In mathematical terms, float is the late finish date minus the early finish date (Figure 12.14).

In the example of three paths in Figure 12.14, only one is the critical path — its float equals zero. The other paths have floats of "3" and "2." The definition of critical path is: the longest, timewise, path through the network and the shortest time in which all the paths of the network (project) can be completed and the path with minimum float. The definition requires a closer look. The first part (longest timewise ...) means just what it says; some interpret this wrongly as the "longest path of activities." The second part (shortest time ...) requires an emphasis on "all the paths." Because the critical path is one of the paths, the critical path establishes both the longest and shortest time to complete the project. The third part (the path with minimum ...) requires additional explanation. Some literature says that "A critical path is the path with zero float." A "zero float" statement is true only when you have applied no constraints to the endpoint date (as shown in the previous example). However, a condition of no constraints on the endpoint is infrequent. More often, a project has a constraint endpoint that is less than the endpoint (EF) established by the team.

In the example in Figure 12.15, a constrained endpoint date of "15" is applied. The critical path that had a "0" float now has a "–2 float." The other paths have similar

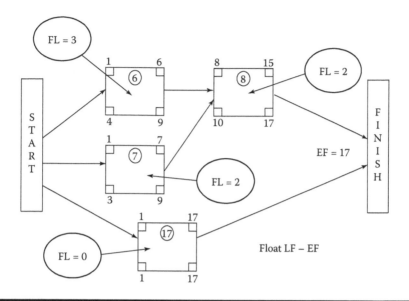

**Figure 12.14   Float.**

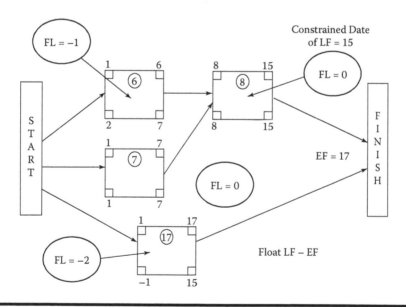

**Figure 12.15   A constrained endpoint.**

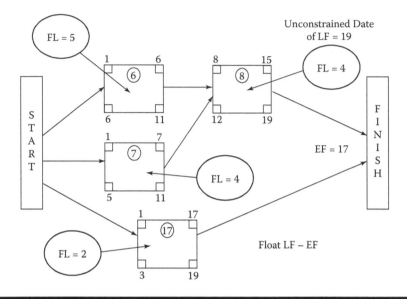

**Figure 12.16   An unconstrained endpoint.**

decreases in their float and now all the paths are critical — there is no leeway in the timing (schedule) of the project. In this case, you could say that "the project is late before it got started."

It is possible for the targeted endpoint to be later than that established by the team — that is, unconstrained (Figure 12.16). Here, the critical path has a float of "+2." The other paths have floats of "+5" and "+4." This is infrequent but can happen. Experience tells us that the team's endpoint most often exceeds the constrained date.

## *Different Floats*

There are two types of floats. The one just described is the *total float*. The other is the *free float* (FFL). The free float is the amount of time an activity can be delayed before its path is delayed. In its simplest interpretation, only the last activity in any path has free float — it has the entire float. (See Figure 12.17.)

Figure 12.18 demonstrates the concept of free float. The only activity that has free float is the last activity on the top row (FFL = 2).

This fact becomes important when using an activity's float to adjust (allocate) the schedule. If the schedule is delayed for either of the two serial activities, their mutual path is delayed. (See Figure 12.19.)

As you can see, if you delay the early start of the first activity, the entire path's schedule changes. This is especially important if the last activity's schedule or resource has been committed for the original early start and early finish dates. Consider free float carefully when performing resource allocation.

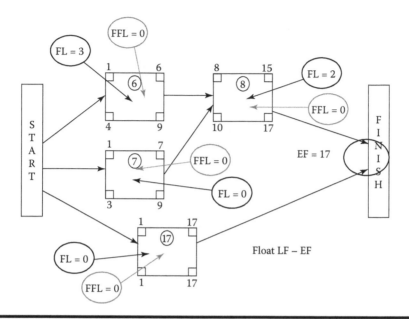

**Figure 12.17    Free float.**

Experience tells us that team members should not be aware of their late dates and their float. If team members know their float, they might view it as a parameter that *they* can modify. They need to understand that unless their activity is last in the path, they will affect everyone (activities) that follows them. A valuable project policy is: *team members are scheduled to the early dates, are not aware of their activity's float, and cannot modify their scheduled dates without consulting with the project manager.*

## Resource Allocation

The network's logic should be based on a very important assumption: *assume unlimited resources.* This assumption may require your team to apply manual resource allocation during CPA. Very often, you will find a number of activities starting at the same time. This causes a "column" of activities with the same early start dates but with perhaps different early finish dates.

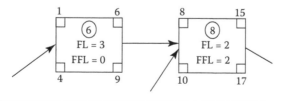

**Figure 12.18    Free float concept.**

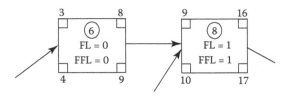

**Figure 12.19  Mutual path is delayed.**

In the example in Figure 12.20, all four activities can begin at the same early start date but their contribution to the critical path would *only be* the 12 days of the bottom activity. The assumption of unlimited resources can allow the construction of this column of activities. However, if 12 days is used for the CPA, the length of the critical path will be incorrect. In this very special case, your team will have to decide how many resources they will need and apply that to the "column" as if it was a single activity.

This now "combined" column (Figure 12.21) will require *2 resources* and *18 days* to complete. When used in CPA, its contribution is now 18 rather than only 12 days' duration. This simple *resource allocation* will adjust the schedule but will not modify the network's logic. PC software can manage a full application of resource allocation.

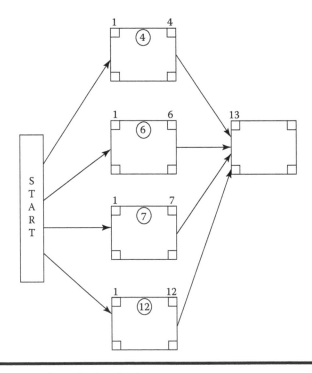

**Figure 12.20  A "column" of activities.**

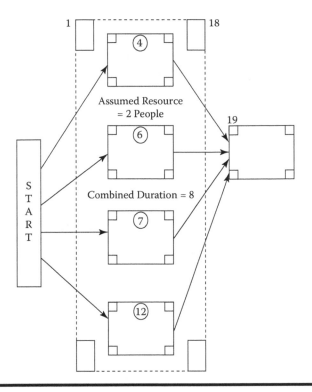

**Figure 12.21    This now "combined" column.**

## *Different Critical Paths*

There are, in fact, three critical paths:

1. The mathematical critical path
2. The near-critical path
3. The perceived critical path

The *mathematical critical path* is the one most often referred to when using the term "critical path." This critical path is the one just demonstrated and if uncon- strained, its float is equal to zero. The *near-critical path* is any path with a float very close to the float of the mathematical critical path. This path (a float path) is important when using your project plan to track progress.

Most PC software can be set to distinguish between the critical path (float = 0) and a "near-critical path" (float = some positive number). This feature is useful when project managers are determining how best apply their management efforts — always "watch" the *critical path* and occasionally "watch" the *near-critical path*.

The *perceived critical path* is an entirely different matter. If your organization, specifically your manager, has experience with your type of project, he or she will develop a *perception of what the critical path should be* — that is, the perceived critical path. To your management, perception is reality. This issue becomes important when your mathematical critical path is significantly different from previous (similar) projects. Experience tells us that if such a condition should occur, your management is "duty bound" to ask, "Why the difference?" *Then and right then,* you must be prepared to articulate the reasons — know the difference before you present your project schedule (plan) to your management. To fail in answering that question can cause severe damage to your credibility.

## Show Your Work

A great deal of the CPA change can occur during Step 8 and again when we execute the second pass. Experience tells us to "show our work" — meaning do not erase any CPA dates but instead mark them and apply the new CPA dates (Figure 12.22).

You are now ready to facilitate your planning session's Step 8.

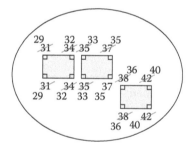

**Figure 12.22   Show your work.**

## Let's Practice

Everything is ready for CPA, and the team performs CPA with very little instruction. The resulting critical path (Figure 12.23) is about what we expected.

The overall project duration is within five days of the target endpoint (on the short side). You (the reader) cannot see the detail, but the critical path (now shown as dotted lines) goes through the generation and approval of subcontractors' contracts. We "work" the critical path and reduce its duration, but now we have two critical paths (Figure 12.24). The second critical path is the negotiations and contracting process with the county board of directors — in this example, we are using a county softball field and associated parking for the event.

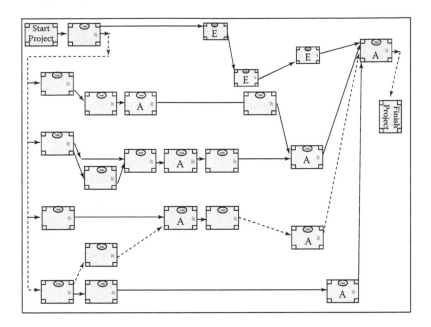

**Figure 12.23   The resulting critical path.**

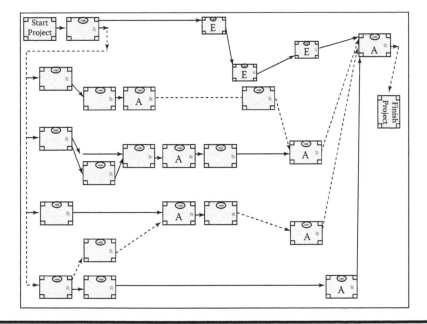

**Figure 12.24   We now have two critical paths.**

## Specific Facilitation Instructions

We now are going to validate our project's timeline (endpoint date) by performing critical path analysis (CPA). Your activities must connect either to another activity or to the finishing activity. Your Post-Its should contain all the necessary information and should look like Figure 12.25.

You begin by performing the *forward pass* of CPA. The four corner boxes will ultimately contain schedule information; but for now, write your calculations just off the Post-Its' corners on the paper, as in Figure 12.26.

The four designations are early start (ES), early finish (EF), late start (LS), and late finish (LF). During the forward pass of CPA, the early dates are calculated (those across the top); and during the backward pass, the late dates are calculated (across the bottom).

As we perform CPA, there will be times when you will recalculate the dates. In this case, do *not* erase the old dates; just mark them out and record the new dates beside or above the old dates (Figure 12.27).

This allows us to show our work and demonstrate our efforts to reduce the overall project duration.

You begin by assigning the early start date of '1' to all starting activities (those calling for 'start activity' as a predecessor) (Figure 12.28).

The mathematics of CPA are simple and you will not need a calculator. The equation for a finish-to-start

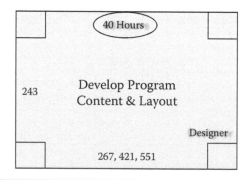

**Figure 12.25   Post-Its with all the necessary information.**

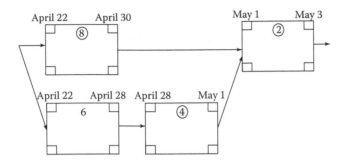

**Figure 12.26   Early dates off the corner.**

relationship is: EF = ES + Duration − 1. Each of the first activities is calculated and the results are their respective early finish (EF). The early finish date is then incremented by one, and it now becomes the early start date for any following activity.

In the example in Figure 12.29, 46 + 3 − 1 = 48 (the early finish date for the first activity). This early finish date then is incremented by 1 and 49 becomes the early start date for the next activity. In turn, the second activity has an early finish date of 56 (49 + 8 − 1 = 56). Please note that this algorithm is for a finish-to-start relationship only. The "−1" accounts for the intervals (Figure 12.30). The increment of '1' between the activities accounts for the fact that you begin your workday interval in the morning — say, 8:30 a.m.

If you have several activities called as predecessors, then the latest early finish is incremented by one and it becomes the early start date. In this example in Figure 12.31, the latest early finish date of '35 + 1'

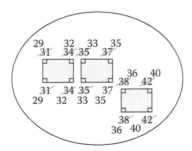

**Figure 12.27   Show your work.**

Forward Pass:

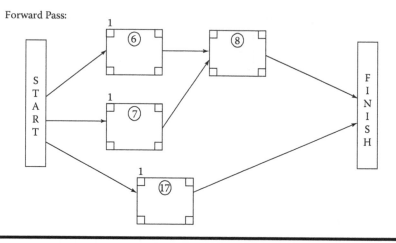

**Figure 12.28 Early start date of "1."**

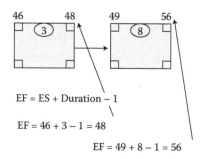

EF = ES + Duration − 1

EF = 46 + 3 − 1 = 48

EF = 49 + 8 − 1 = 56

**Figure 12.29 Forward pass.**

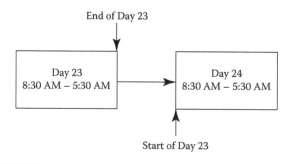

**Figure 12.30 The "−1" accounts for the intervals.**

becomes the early start date (36) for the activity.

A more complicated diagram such as that in Figure 12.32 might help you better understand CPA. The final early finish date becomes the early finish date (17) for the Network (project). The forward pass calculates the earliest the activities can start and finish.

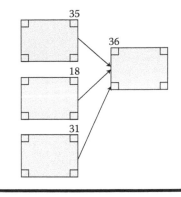

**Figure 12.31    The "sink" activity.**

The backward pass begins with the *early finish date* calculated by the forward pass. This is the earliest the entire project can be finished based on the logic of the Network and the durations of the activities. The calculations for the backward pass are simply the reverse of the forward pass. When you added the duration for the forward pass, you now subtract it. When you incremented by one for forward pass, you now decrement by one. When you take the latest early finish for many activities into a single activity for the forward pass, you now take the earliest late start back into a single activity (Figure 12.33).

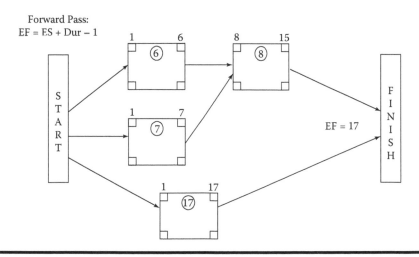

**Figure 12.32    A more complicated diagram.**

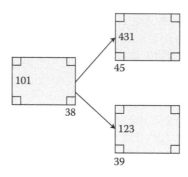

**Figure 12.33   A sink for the backward pass.**

The backward pass uses the EF date calculated during the forward pass and calculates the latest any activity can start and finish (Figure 12.34).

Once you have calculated both directions in the network, you are ready to calculate the float for each activity. The definition of float is the amount of time you can delay the start of an activity before you delay the project. The calculation of float is part of the mathematics of CPA. In mathematical terms, float is the late finish date minus the early finish date (Figure 12.35).

In the example of three paths in Figure 12.35, only one is the critical path — its float equals zero. The other paths

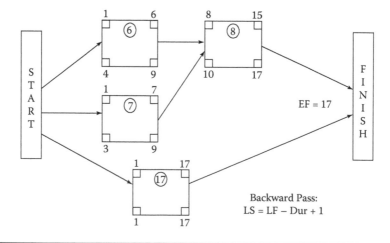

**Figure 12.34   The backward pass calculation.**

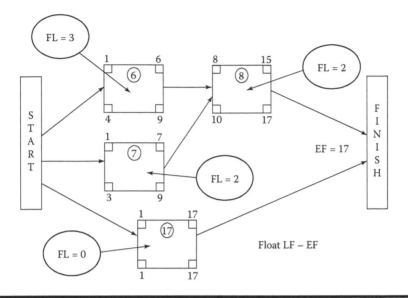

**Figure 12.35   Float.**

have floats of '3' and '2.' The definition of critical path is the longest, timewise, path through the network and the shortest time in which all the paths of the network (project) can be completed and the path with minimum float. We need the float to determine those paths that are critical and will require special attention.

A condition can occur that will require you to perform manual resource allocation. Remember that you formed your network's logic on a very important assumption: assume unlimited resources. This assumption may require you now to apply resource allocation during CPA. Very often, you will find that a number of activities can all start at the same time. This causes a 'column' of activities with the same early start but with perhaps different early finish dates (Figure 12.36).

In this special case (Figure 12.36), these four activities can all begin at the same date (1) and their contribution to the critical path would be *only* the '12' days — that is, the duration of the bottom activity.

The assumption of unlimited resources created the logic but will now cause an error in the length of the

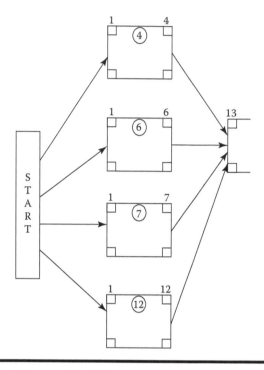

**Figure 12.36   A "column" of activities.**

critical path. In this case, you must decide how many resources you need and apply that to the 'column' as if it was a single activity. This now 'combined' column (Figure 12.37) is assumed to require '2' resources and '18' days to complete. When used in CPA, its contribution is now '18' rather than only '12.' This process of adjusting the schedule and not the network logic is known as resource allocation. PC software can manage a full application of resource allocation.

Now is the time to perform CPA. It will work best if you form a team of at least two people. One person performs the calculations and the other checks his or her results. This checking is necessary because the calculated dates are cumulative, and any error will distort the endpoint date. Remember to show your work. After you have finished the CPA, highlight your critical path (there may be multiple critical paths). In addition, there is a tendency to make changes (in logic and durations)

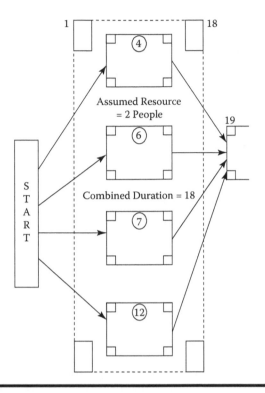

**Figure 12.37 This now "combined" column.**

during CPA. Make note of needed changes, but *do not make any changes* until we perform the 'second pass.'
Checklist:

- Show your work (off the corners).
- Make no changes in logic or durations during this step.
- Calculate the critical path in both directions.
- Highlight the critical path (paths).
- If an activity column occurs, calculate it as a resource allocated group.

This step is time boxed for XX minutes. If you have any questions, I will be here — please ask them.

Otherwise, let's go to work!

## Hints

### Observe and Note

During Step 8, you can gather valuable information concerning your team: how they work together and who leads the team under stress. Observe the CPA process for this information and "note" it for yourself.

## Tendency to Make Changes

You already have warned your team not to make changes during CPA. This will be important as you validate the project timeline. Any changes made now will require rework of the CPA. Reserve your changes for the second pass. Your full attention will be necessary to enforce this policy.

## The Second Pass

When you perform this step for the second pass, your team will be experienced in CPA. Now you can direct your full attention to the endpoint date — check the CPA calculation for yourself.

## First Pass and Backward CPA

If your network is not complicated and not large, you need perform only the forward pass. The forward pass will reveal the critical path (paths) — the paths requiring further attention during the second pass.

## CPA and the Project's Target Date

In most cases, your project's endpoint date is, in fact, a calendar date. However, CPA provides the "absolute" working dates (days) and it does not provide the endpoint as a calendar date. To translate absolute dates into a "rough" calendar date, you can use an average of "21" days per month and calculate your endpoint date (Figure 12.38). This simple calculation will give you a "rough" estimate of your project's endpoint date but now as a *calendar date*.

> Your CPA is calculated to be 128 absolute working days
>
> if there is an average of 21 working days per month
>
> Then the project could take 6 months
>
> Start the project on April 15th and it could be
>
> finished on October 15th.

**Figure 12.38   Use an average of "21" days per month.**

## Big Problem or Error?

Occasionally, CPA will produce a very, very high value for the endpoint date. Before getting upset, check the mathematics of your team's CPA. Experience tells us that a very, very high endpoint date can result from one very common error. During CPA, an error can occur if the team uses a unique identifier (UI) as the duration. If the UI is 434 and the duration is two (2) days, your project endpoint just became 432 days too long. This is the reason the duration is circled and UIs start with a three-digit number — no activity should ever have three-digit duration.

On the other hand, if the mathematics check out as good, you will need to perform extensive analysis of your network logic and the individual durations to reduce the project's duration.

## When to Use PC Software

If you find that your network is extremely large (more than 200 activities), you may not be able to assemble the entire network on a single space (wall). If this should happen, you should consider using PC software to combine it and calculate the critical path. This is not the ideal situation but it may be necessary.

If you sense that this condition will occur, you can soften the impact by carrying out some advance work. Begin data entry (PC software) as soon as possible and in stages. Enter the activities and their UIs after Step 4 and the project's logic (as predecessors) after Step 5. Enter the resources after Step 6 and the durations as developed in Step 7. In this way, you will have everything entered in your PC software to perform Step 8. One problem with this idea concerns who performs data entry. If *you* enter the data, then *who* leads the team and keeps the Process going? Consider hiring and deploying a data entry person who knows your PC software — and thus that problem is solved.

## When Not to Use PC Software

The use of PC software at this point in the Process is not advisable because of its effect on the team effort. Picture the following scenario. Your planning team has worked hard and long to get through Step 7 and you now begin data entry on your PC. The question is: what does your team do while you are hammering away on the PC? Experience tells us that they tune out, disengage, and generally disappear. Without your team, you will have a very difficult time solving problems related to confusing logic, too long durations, missing activities, etc. The very people who could have helped, have all left — either physically or mentally. Make every effort to avoid using PC software during Step 8.

## Keep Their Attention

It is amazing how CPA maintains the attention of your planning team. The question is: why are they so interested in the endpoint date of the project? They are, of course, interested in the endpoint date but their interest really lies in whether their activities are on the critical path, will they occur during their planned vacation, or they will affect other committed projects. They are interested most in what affects them personally.

## What Are You Changing Now?

It is truly amazing to observe team members as they watch the CPA dates unfold. In most cases, the full team will physically follow and watch the team members performing CPA. They are following closely to see where their activities "fall." If you do not watch them carefully and warn them against it, they will start making dynamic, unconsidered changes to their activities' logic and durations. Any changes during CPA will only invalidate the CPA just performed. You could let this happen as an alternative to performing a second pass, but it (the dynamic changes) would be unorganized and chaotic. Establish the following during your instructions:

1. Clearly establish that there will be a *second pass* to allow for changes to their activity's durations and logic.
2. Ask them to observe the calculations but *make no changes at this time*.

## Do Not Schedule Yet

It is possible that you could schedule the activities' dates after you perform CPA, but fight the urge. The simple mathematics of "average working days per month" should be adequate to validate your endpoint date. If you schedule at this time, there is a high probability that the resulting schedule dates will be "locked in" (people's memory) before the dates are fully analyzed, tested, and stabilized.

# POST-PLANNING ACTIVITIES

# Chapter 13

# Second Pass

## Why a Second Pass?

A second pass is simply going back into the Process at Step 3 (Figure 13.1).

During the second pass, you will lead your team back again through Step 3 through Step 8. This second pass will allow the project team to refine its activity description, predecessors, order of activities (network logic), assigned person, and duration. You have been promoting the second pass all through the Process, and it is now time to execute. Your team will value this process as a second chance to adjust its planning and try alternative paths through the Network.

### Adjust the Timings

You will value it because it will provide you with an opportunity to tighten the "timing parameters" of the project. A key timing parameter is the maximum duration of any activity on a critical path. You probably have not taken any position on this parameter yet and, in fact, you have let it "float to a natural level." It is now time to express your expectations regarding durations on the critical path.

### New Rules

During the Process, you asked your team members for durations without any rules for maximum durations. It was not necessary to set any timing parameter for duration. You only needed a "sampling" of the *probable durations* to calculate the critical path. Now that you know the critical path, you need to apply a common-sense rule to the maximum duration of any activity on the critical path. This rule

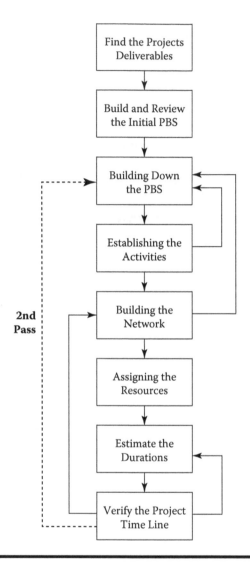

**Figure 13.1 A second pass: back into the process at Step 3.**

will establish for your team the duration variance (plus/minus days) that the project (and you) can tolerate. As an example, say your project is 12 months long and the client has an expectation for completion, minus no earlier than (minus nothing) and no later than two weeks (+2 weeks). This is the variance as the project begins. Therefore, you cannot have any activity on the critical path with duration longer than two weeks. The reasoning is that if an activity's duration is three weeks and it is late, then you will be one week beyond the client's expected date before you even know you are late. If, on the other hand, an activity's duration is only one week and it is late, you will still be within the variance of the client's expected date. You will have to determine your project's variance range and apply it during the second pass.

## New Rule Applied and Added Value

This new duration rule takes the form a policy statement: "No activity on a critical path can have a duration that exceeds five days." This rule can force some unexpected added value. Because each activity is producing a deliverable, this policy will force the assigned person to redefine the deliverable. Frequently, this redefinition results in a series of smaller deliverables (decomposed) and resulting smaller duration activities. Experience tells us that two additional possibilities occur by the creation of a series of now-shorter activities: (1) the sum of the activities' durations can sometimes be less than the original, longer activity; and (2) the series can prompt different logic, turning a series of activities into alternate, parallel paths. In both cases, there can be a reduction in the overall duration along the critical path. The policy has created for the project manager finer control (more frequent, shorter activities) over the critical path — that is added value!

## Another Timing Parameter

The other timing parameter is the project's endpoint date. If your team has met or bettered the date, no official effort to reduce it is necessary. However, experience tells us that the schedule success of a project lies in the ability of the team to not only "make the date" but *to better it*. During the second pass, you have an opportunity to set up the conditions to better the endpoint date. This is the time to build into the project schedule extra durations before the target endpoint — a buffer. There are many ways to accomplish the buffer but a more important consideration is "what you call the buffer." If you do call it "buffer," it will probably have a short life: it will be "stripped out" by your management. However, if properly named, it could actually survive any such attack. A buffer named Quality Assurance Review or Client's Review will have a far better chance of survival. Any such buffer will force the actual project's endpoint date back in time. This unofficial endpoint date has many different names — team target, understood date, stretch date, etc.

# Kickoff

Usually by now, your team has the endpoint date in view and they understand the rules of the game. If not, then restate your intention to repeat Step 3 through Step 8 again and that the emphasis will be the critical path. Try to create a climate of anything goes — "just try it and let's see the results." The second pass will typically require only one third the time that the Process required — but do not hurry it.

# Chapter 14

# Manual Scheduling

You have now finished all eight steps of the Process and you have a decision to make: how should I schedule the project? You either can manually establish a calendar date for each activity or you can use PC software for your project. The answer is simple if you wish to provide closure to your project team. Your team has worked hard and long developing the project plan. By rough calculations, your endpoint date is within your team's capability. You could either "turn them loose" now or get back with them later on the specific dates for their activities. In terms of member morale, you could provide closure on their need for knowing these dates now and before they exit the Session. There is a simple answer: do it now, manually!

## Shop Calendar

You will manually schedule your project with a shop calendar (Figure 14.1), a simple tool that numbers the workdays of your project sequentially, starting with the first day of your project.

The fragment of a shop calendar in Figure 14.1 will work just fine for the task of scheduling the individual activities. The numbers in the left column are the absolute days your team entered on the Network as they calculated the critical path. The dates in the right column are the calendar dates that would correspond with a target start date of the first of July. To schedule an activity, you find the absolute date of interest and the corresponding calendar date.

## Early Start

Using the shop calendar, find the absolute dates of those penciled on the paper just off the corners. Then write the corresponding dates on the upper-left corners of the Post-Its®. For example, the absolute date of 34 translates into the calendar date of August 15 (Figure 14.2).

## Early Finishes

Now find the absolute date for the early finish. The corresponding calendar day is August 19. Write in the early finish day in the upper-right corner box (Figure 14.3).

After scheduling the Network, review the dates for reasonableness in regard to the target endpoint date.

| ABS. Days | Date |
|-----------|------|
| 34 | 8/15 |
| 35 | 8/18 |
| 36 | 8/19 |
| 37 | 8/20 |
| 38 | 8/21 |
| 39 | 8/22 |
| 40 | 8/25 |
| | |

**Figure 14.1  Shop calendar.**

# Float

If you have performed the backward pass, schedule the late dates and calculate the activity's float. Write the float on each activity, to the right of the duration (Figure 14.4).

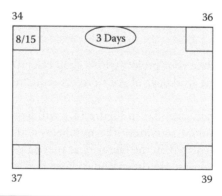

**Figure 14.2  The calendar date of August 15.**

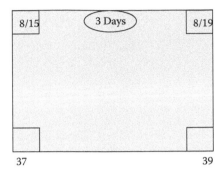

**Figure 14.3  Write in the early finish day.**

## Hint

Experience tells us that scheduling a complicated network can be tedious and prone to errors. To reduce the tedium and to keep the team engaged, have everyone on the team participate; one member calls the numbers, all members write their own dates on their Post-Its, and everyone checks his or her own work! The project's shop calendar is built in advance by a team member: look for someone who is about to "tune out." All team members will require a copy of the project's shop calendar.

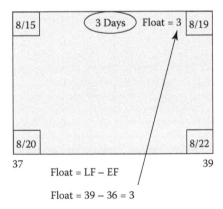

**Figure 14.4  Write the float.**

# Chapter 15

# Scheduled Network

## Background

The scheduled network is built from the original Network. The result is a network that is scheduled in calendar dates. The result is a hybrid between a network and a Gantt chart.

This Gantt chart in Figure 15.1 shows four activities (A, B, C, D) as bars arranged according to their early start dates (4/22, 4/28, 5/03). The length of the bars (activities) varies according to the duration of the activity, and each line of the chart contains only one activity (as a bar). This Gantt chart is very common as an output of PC software.

There are two differences between the Gantt chart in Figure 15.1 and the chart you will be building: (1) the length of the bars will not vary, and (2) each line can contain multiple activities (Post-Its®) (Figure 15.2).

### PC Software versus Manual

During the construction of your network, it is possible that you also have been using PC software. The difficulty with PC software is the output formats and the printer or plotter limit physical report sizes. However, a combination of the visual schedule you are about to create and the textual reports from the PC software provides you with both the choice and the means to implement your plan and to communicate project progress, either manually or by computer. You also can combine methods, using your visual project schedule as a form of progress reporting and your computer to generate textual reports.

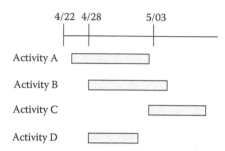

**Figure 15.1    A Gantt chart.**

## Clean It Up

Review the appearance of the Network. Would you be proud to present it outside your project team? Would you be proud to show it to your chief executive officer? If the answer is no, you need to clean up the Network. First, does it have a smooth flow from left to right and with no loop-backs? Second, is there any missing scheduling — upper corners of the Post-Its? If you want to keep the Network intact, make duplicate Post-Its for each activity and stick them over the original Post-Its: the duplicates will become the activity bars for your scheduled network chart.

## Lay Out the Gantt Chart

We will assume that you want to keep the Network intact and you will be using banner paper.

Start your scheduled network chart by laying out a clean sheet of banner paper (about six feet long) on a convenient wall. Draw a horizontal line across the paper and about three inches down from the top edge, but do not write on it yet. This line will become your project timeline. Now collect the duplicate Post-Its according to early start dates. Collect all the duplicate Post-Its with the same early start date (Figure 15.3). This should leave you with piles of Post-Its. These piles represent the possible early start dates. Arrange all Post-Its with the earliest early start on the left edge of your banner paper. Mark this early date on the timeline on the top of the banner paper.

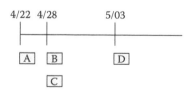

**Figure 15.2    Each line contains multiple activities.**

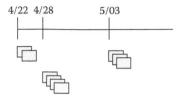

**Figure 15.3 Collect all the duplicate Post-Its.**

Now arrange the Post-Its with the next early start date. Continue with the preceding steps until all your Post-Its are placed (Figure 15.4).

Once you have all your Post-Its arranged, pencil in the relationships indicated as predecessors on the Post-Its (Figure 15.5). Then look for opportunities to move your Post-Its so that you minimize the number of lines that cross over one another (Figure 15.6).

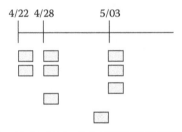

**Figure 15.4 All Post-Its are placed.**

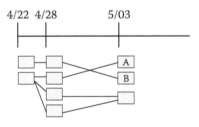

**Figure 15.5 Pencil in the relationships.**

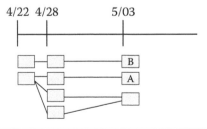

**Figure 15.6 Minimize the number of cross-over lines.**

## *Other Orders*

You could, of course, "order" your Post-Its by any of the other dates (EF, LS, and LF). However, using the early start dates will help your project team concentrate on their early dates. When you have all your Post-Its on the banner paper, step back and see if any rearrangement of the Post-Its would improve the overall look. Some people like to "zone" this type of chart, or place a particular type of organization or work in the same horizontal zone or band. Although it may look appealing, this can be difficult to achieve and maintaining the zones is sure to drive you crazy.

After spending some time analyzing your scheduled network, stop changing it. Try to maintain the "look" of the original chart you presented to management — it is the view they will remember. Now darken the pencil lines with a pen.

## Where to Put the Scheduled Network

You will want to find a good place to post your chart. Try to find a location in your project team meeting room. It is best to place a small amount of transparent tape on top of each Post-It — time, dust, and humidity are not kind to them. You might consider covering your chart with a plastic cover for added protection.

# Chapter 16

# Tracking and Reporting

## Keeping Track of Progress

Your chart is ready now for progress tracking and reporting. Progress tracking has two parts: (1) tracking and (2) analysis. The frequency of tracking and reporting is set by your project control cycle (Figure 16.1).

The project control cycle is the lapse time between statuses reporting. This is a simple version of the project control cycle. It emphasizes the detection of changes or significant differences from your project plan (schedule). The project control cycle begins with your developed plan. First, you communicate your plan and then implementation begins. You begin immediately to track and report actual activity starts and finishes. You analyze your results and test for significant differences against your plan. Continue your cycle of reporting if you are satisfied that you have no significant differences. If you detect significant differences, you will need to refresh your plan. This refresh is different from a planned refresh. These plan refreshes are necessary because your planned activities and your actual activities are significantly different.

What is significantly different? Significant differences take on many different "forms." They could be when activities are starting out of sequence — without their predecessors' activities completed first. A significant difference can occur when activities that should have started have not started, and the person assigned does not know when they will start. A significant difference can occur when late activities cannot be recovered by extraordinary effort. These are only examples of what a significant difference might be.

As you gain experience, you will begin to recognize situations that tell you when it is time to refresh your project plan. Real-life project situations that vary from the project plan are natural and normal. If you think the project will execute exactly according to plan — that is abnormal and unnatural. It is a fact of project

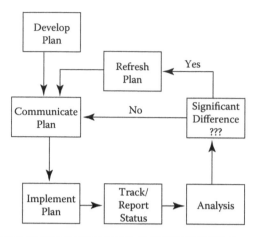

**Figure 16.1   Project control cycle.**

life that the plan-to-actual differences start to occur immediately after the Session is complete; the project plan is only an estimate of what might occur.

Because of their close involvement in the plan's development, your project team will understand how they interconnect with other team members. This understanding will help them either execute their activities as planned or inform you (the project manager) of necessary changes. You can establish this frank relationship by your constant emphasis on the plan's schedule and on your insistence that they plan their work and work their plan.

## *Who Reports Actual Performance?*

Who provides the actual chart entry of tracking information? The single most error-prone option occurs if you allow the responsible person to report his or her own progress on the chart. On the other hand, this method is the most satisfying to your team members. Consider another option: one individual (perhaps you) reports all progress. If you elect this option, that one person (you?) will be expected to report all progress for the project team and to answer all the questions. It certainly is a way to appear to be in control, but again, the maximum satisfaction for the project members is achieved when they report their own status.

## *An Additional Value of Progress Reporting*

Reporting both the start and finish of an activity is essential to the project team's understanding of (1) the value of the plan and (2) your reliance on their reporting integrity. By reporting "project starts," the assigned person is focusing on getting their activity off *as planned* and on the "right foot." By reporting "project finishes,"

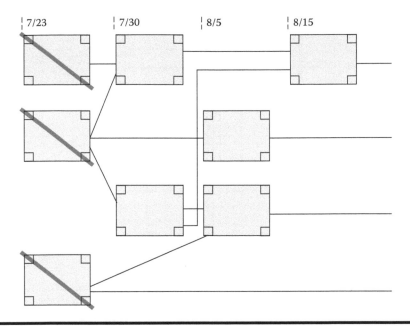

**Figure 16.2   Reporting project starts.**

the same person is completing their progress cycle and assuring you that they have in fact completed the activity as agreed.

## Reporting Project Starts

The scheduled network now becomes your media for reporting activity progress. You report an activity's start by drawing a line from the upper left-hand corner to the bottom right-hand corner of the Post-Its® (Figure 16.2).

(*Note:* Experience tells us that using a blue highlighter on a yellow Post-It will result in a green mark — your team might even begin to call this action "greening the chart.")

## Reporting Project Finishes

You report an activity as finished by the same method as above but draw the line from the lower left to upper right-hand corner (Figure 16.3). At this point, you need to analyze your project's progress and take inventory of how the progress is affecting the target endpoint.

## Time-now

Another technique that will help identify progress is to establish a time-now, or the date when progress is sampled. This date is generally a few days to a week before a

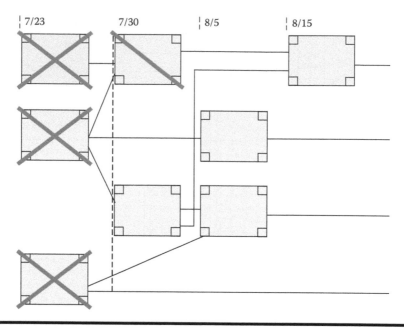

**Figure 16.3    Reporting project finishes.**

project review. Try to minimize this delay between when progress is sampled and reported.

Establish the time-now with a line on the chart (Figure 16.4). The line must be moveable — use a piece of red string weighted by a fishing sinker and tacked to the top of the chart. The line can thus move across the chart as the time-now date changes.

## Other Uses

It is interesting to see how your team can use the tracking chart. It allows them to sense how the project is progressing without getting into the detail — from as far as ten feet away. What they will look for is activities to the left of the time-now line that have not started. This cues them to move in for details on a particular activity. They can tell the activity has not started because of a missing (now green) line from the upper left to bottom right corner. Your management also will display considerable interest in activities that are scheduled to start and are not yet reported started.

## Analysis

If you decide to allow team members to report their own progress, you must review their progress before they have posted their results; never fail to perform this

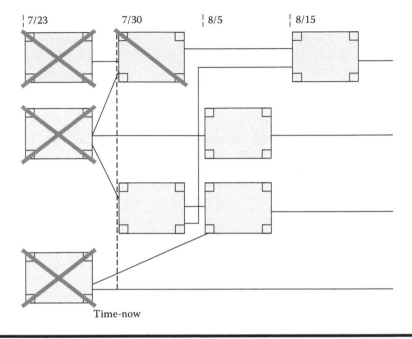

**Figure 16.4   Time-now.**

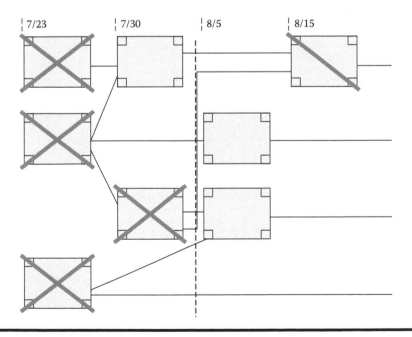

**Figure 16.5   Activities performed out of sequence.**

analysis for yourself. Look for activities performed out of sequence (Figure 16.5) to get a hint that the plan may not be realistic, and then review this with the assigned person. Next, look for activities started before their predecessors have been reported as either finished or started.

For example, notice that the activity in the upper-right corner of Figure 16.5 has been reported as "started" out of sequence. This activity cannot be reported as started until all its predecessors have not been reported as finished.

Experience tells us that when the assigned person reports their own progress, they tend to be more careful that their report is factual and timely. They take ownership of their portion of the scheduled network chart.

# Chapter 17

## Resource Allocation

### Rough Cut

After manually scheduling the activities, you will be able to perform a "rough cut" at resource allocation. It will be a *rough cut* because if there are a number of very complicated resource situations, you will need PC software to manage them.

### *Review the Situation*

Resource allocation is simply a review of the individual team member's personal commitments and previous business constraints. Individuals can generally sense when they have schedule mismatch with other projects to which they have already committed. The easiest way to see a resource allocation situation is to follow the scheduled network chart. What you are looking for is activities assigned to the same person and starting on the same date (Figure 17.1).

Here you can see that Mike must start both activities 360 and 240 on July 15. This date was established by critical path analysis and the assumption that Mike had "unlimited resources." It is also possible the policy that activities cannot have a duration shorter than one day caused this situation.

There are a number of approaches to solve this problem; but when presented with a situation requiring resource allocation, you should follow a process logically (Figure 17.2).

You can first determine if the logic should be rearranged by the first question (Is the logic correct?). The second question can start resource allocation to start

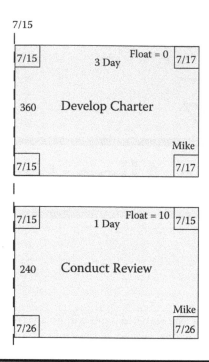

**Figure 17.1   Activities assigned to the same person.**

(Do any activities have float?) by determining whether there are activities not on the critical path. If the second question results in a "yes," then the third question determines whether there is adequate float for rescheduling the activity. If the answer is "no," then you will need to find another resource to relieve the situation. These three questions and their answers (and the "side" questions) then allow resource allocation to occur.

The application of this logical process would result in a rescheduling of Mike's activities (Figure 17.3). Now activity 240 is rescheduled to July 18 and it still has a float of seven (7) days. This is a simple example but it does demonstrate the process you must perform.

Resource allocation is the adjusting of the activities scheduled days to assign a limited resource. That limited resource can be any kind of resource. In this example, it is human. In general, begin with the activities (and resources) early on the critical path. Major rearrangements of the logic and schedules are most successful in the next 25 percent (as time) of the critical path. Beyond that time limit, the critical path can change significantly, and any efforts taken now could

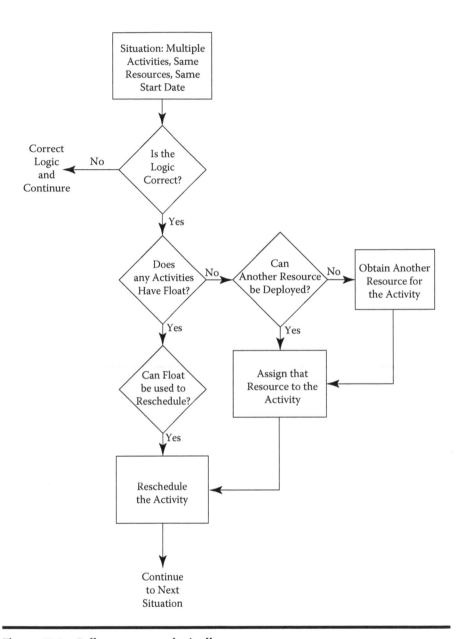

**Figure 17.2   Follow a process logically.**

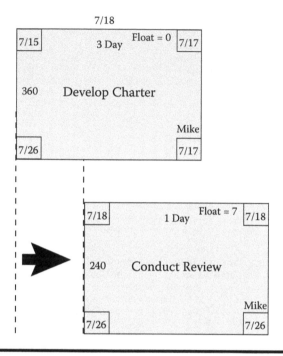

**Figure 17.3  Rescheduling Mike's activities.**

easily be made invalid by a change. Spend the time to perform resource allocation on the timeframe you know the most about — your window of knowledge. Experience tells us that manual resource allocation is easy for any one resource (assigned person). Also, it is very worthwhile if performed while that particular person is present. PC software should be used for resource allocation of complicated networks.

# SOME BASIC PROJECT MANAGEMENT ISSUES

**IV**

# Chapter 18

# Let's Practice
# Case Study Summary

## Step 1

We can use the case study to practice. Your assignment of this special event happens very simply in a note from your boss (Figure 18.1a). This note is all you have to start the project. Your boss is the head of research and he wants you to plan a one-day recognition event. Let's circle the deliverables he has described thus far (Figure 18.1b). There is not much here, but it is a beginning.

Now look at some meeting notes you made a few days later (Figure 18.2). This document is beginning to reveal the client's expectations. Let's now highlight the additional deliverables he has just described (Figure 18.3)

This was a good start, but now we need more definition for the employees and spouses. The next day you meet and document that meeting (Figure 18.4). Now find the added deliverables — some are hiding (Figure 18.5).

You highlight "spouses" as a noun but upon further analysis, you decide that "spouses" is not a deliverable. This is the general process of finding and evaluating the project's deliverables. You now finish Step 1 by writing out a Post-It for each highlighted deliverable.

## Step 2: Part One (Build)

You decide how to organize the first level of your initial PBS (Figure 18.6). As you can see, there is very little depth but is does have some width. This organization will probably require some adjustments later. Once the first level is established, you can start assembling the PBS from the available, defined deliverables (Figure 18.7).

| | |
|---|---|
| Provide a recognition event for 400 employees and their families with programs for adults and children all on one day. | Provide a ⟨recognition event⟩ for 400 employees and their families with ⟨programs⟩ for ⟨adults⟩ and ⟨children⟩ all on one day. |
| (a) | (b) |

**Figure 18.1    (a) A note from your boss; and (b) circle the deliverables.**

Meeting Notes:
Wednesday 5th.

Boss: "I would like good safe programs for the employee's children. There seems to be three categories; teenagers, grade-schoolers, and the very young (maybe even babies).

The teenagers seem interested in only electronic games.

The grade-schooler would probably like physical activities such as event rides and games of skills.

The small children, well, they need to be cared for so their parents can attend the technical program, I guess that's a nursery.

Let's concentrate on defining these (programs) at this time. Let's meet during lunch tomorrow – to discuss the program for the adults.

**Figure 18.2    Some meeting notes.**

Meeting Notes:
Wednesday 5th.

Boss: "I would like good safe programs for the employee's children. There seems to be three categories; teenagers, grade-schoolers, and the very young (maybe even babies).

The teenagers seem interested in only electronic games.

The grade-schooler would probably like physical activities such as event rides and games of skills.

The small children, well, they need to be cared for so their parents can attend the technical program, I guess that's a nursery.

Let's concentrate on defining these (programs) at this time. Let's meet during lunch tomorrow – to discuss the program for the adults.

**Figure 18.3    Highlight the additional deliverables.**

Meeting Notes:
Thursday

Boss: " Let me tell you what I envision for the employee's
program and to a much lesser degree the general
entertainment.

Let's show off our latest patents and how they are helping
the bottom line – demonstrations of how they are applied.
You pick several of the more significant ones. The
demonstration area will have to have special access security
n– employees only.

While we are on that subject – the entire area must have
access control and safety officers in the parking areas.

I want your recommendations on a program for the spouses
and food service next week.

The entertainment must be first rate. You know I
particularly like country western BUT not everyone does.
Find a musical group that can cover them all.

**Figure 18.4    The next day you meet (notes).**

Meeting Notes:
Thursday

Boss: " Let me tell you what I envision for the employee's
program and to a much lesser degree the general
entertainment.

Let's show off our latest patents and how they are helping
the bottom line – demonstrations of how they are applied.
You pick several of the more significant ones. The
demonstration area will have to have special access security
n– employees only.

While we are on that subject – the entire area must have
access control and safety officers in the parking areas.

I want your recommendations on a program for the spouses
and food service next week.

The entertainment must be first rate. You know I
particularly like country western BUT not everyone does.
Find a musical group that can cover them all.

**Figure 18.5    Find the added deliverables.**

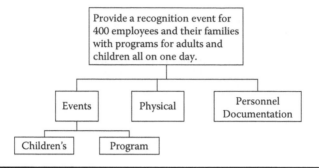

**Figure 18.6  Your initial PBS.**

Further meetings with your boss and event planners help to define additional, more detailed deliverables. The initial PBS now takes on a more complete form (Figure 18.8).

## Step 2: Part Two (Client Presentation)

You prepare by explaining the initial PBS to several people. These advance presentations provide you with notes that are indicative of any presentation gaps (quality of your presentation), their interest (proper depth of your presentation), and their lack of understanding (clarity of your presentation). Your notes help you further refine your presentation by getting you "out ahead" of possible similar questions at the Presentation.

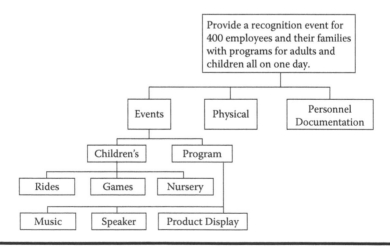

**Figure 18.7  Assembling the PBS.**

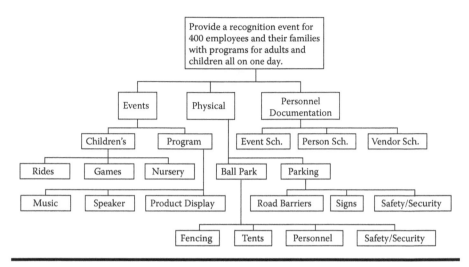

**Figure 18.8   A more complete form.**

# Step 3

You have just returned from the Presentation and a number of deliverables were further defined (Figure 18.9). Your planning session starts in two days and you want more deliverables to "fill out" the PBS. Your history search turns up last year's

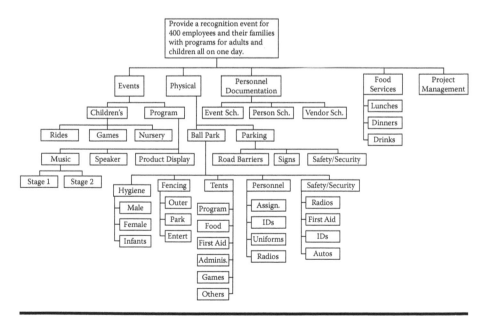

**Figure 18.9   More deliverables defined.**

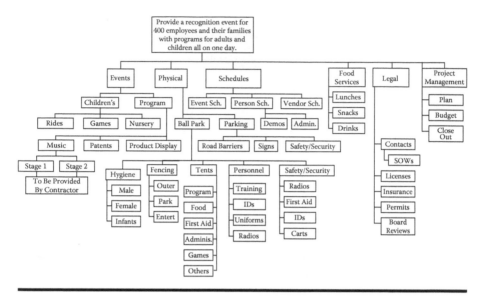

**Figure 18.10   You eliminated several items.**

event project manager, and you engage him for an hour as a subject matter expert. During that meeting, you eliminate several items from the PBS and add a few (Figure 18.10).

At this point, you have expended your knowledge of detail and you are ready to bring on the full project team. The definition of the deliverables is, in most legs, to the fourth level. There were no *client deliverables,* and more than half of the defined deliverables are *process deliverables.* The large content of process deliverables seems justified for a project at this level of detail. It was difficult at times to remember the definition of your assignment: "The project plan is to include only the planning portion and not the actual implementation of the event." The assignment, as defined, is to include deliverables only to the point of starting the event. Thereafter, the individual vendors and implementation teams will be in full control (with their own plans).

## Step 4

You start the Session by reviewing the PBS from Step 3. In general, the team agrees with the items but not necessarily the PBS's organization (you really did not expect them to agree, did you?). After an hour, the team has made some minor rearrangements and added several more deliverables (Figure 18.11).

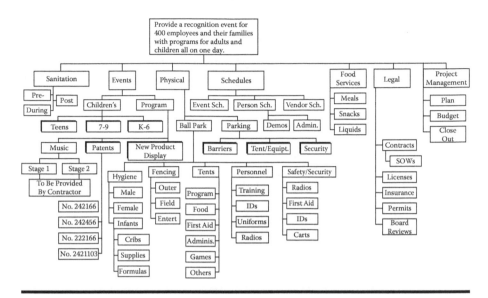

**Figure 18.11   Added several more deliverables.**

They seem pleased with their work result and especially pleased with the result-ing transfer of knowledge. It is evident to you: they have "bought in" *to their newly rearranged PBS.*

Next, you discuss the issue of their window of knowledge. We consider the following facts: (1) the project's overall duration is less than 3 months and (2) they have detail knowledge of the effort involved. Therefore, we decide to plan the entire project at this session and to refresh the plan only once — two weeks before the event.

You pass out supplies, give the necessary instructions, and stand back. Their resulting activities are "posted" on the newly rearranged PBS (Figure 18.12).

When all deliverables were "covered" by activities, we reviewed the possibil-ity of missing deliverables. I instructed them on the concept of "assembly point activities" and, as expected, they found five significant assembly points that would require this type of activity (Figure 18.13).

The team defined the activities for the lower-level assembly points (there were four). You defined the four assembly point activities for the assembly of first-level components into level zero.

There still were some missing activities. Because the "Children's Program" was completely subcontracted, we decided to bring in that subcontractor; after some instruction, the subcontractor will layout its own plan (Figure 18.14).

After adding the vendor's project plan to our project plan, we amended their contract to include their reporting requirements.

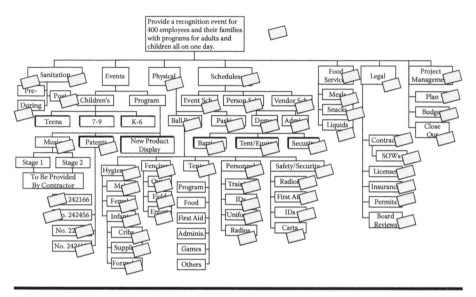

**Figure 18.12  Activities were "posted."**

# Step 5

In Step 4, we developed the activities and placed them over the corresponding deliverables (Figure 18.15).

Because we are a small team, we decide to all work on the same network. We build a work area on the wall with flipchart paper and masking tape. We had

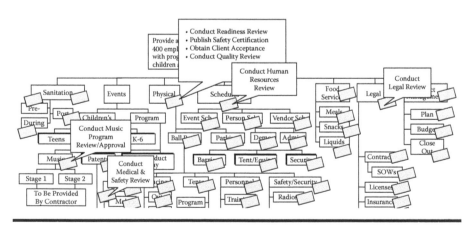

**Figure 18.13  Significant assembly points.**

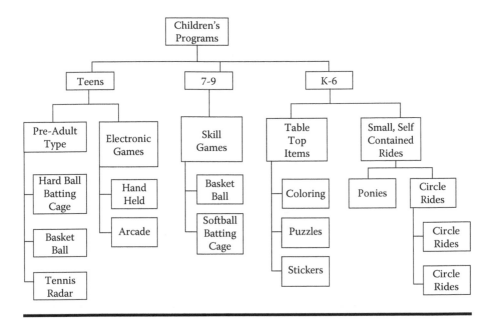

**Figure 18.14   Children's Program.**

forgotten the "Start" and "Finish" activities, so we wrote them out, and placed them in the new work area to begin our network (Figure 18.16).

Next, we place those activities that "organize" a project — kickoff meeting, planning session, budget (money), and schedules (timing) (Figure 18.17).

Then we placed the activities that produce the "process deliverables" (Figure 18.18).

The process deliverables (as activities) form a column because they all can begin at the same time and we have assumed "unlimited resources."

Then the "big bang" occurs — all legs of the deliverables (now as activities) began. However, it was obvious we would quickly run out of room on the work area. We decide to rearrange the network (Figure 18.19).

Now with this new organization, we expand the network with a series of paths representing the four major areas of effort (Figure 18.20).

We continued with higher-level activities and identified assembly point activities (Figure 18.21).

We are essentially complete with these last additions but we decide to include some post-event activities (Figure 18.22).

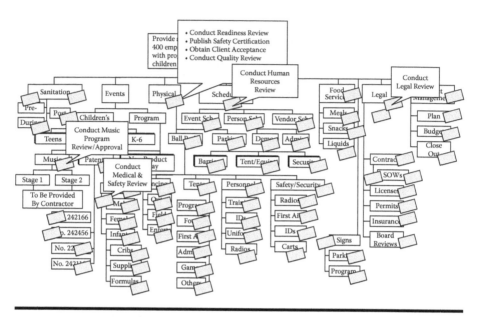

**Figure 18.15  Place Post-Its® over deliverables.**

**Figure 18.16  Begin our network.**

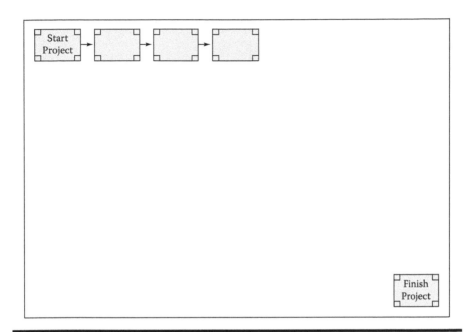

**Figure 18.17    Activities that "organize."**

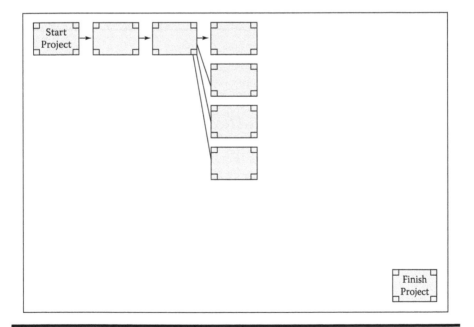

**Figure 18.18    "Process deliverables."**

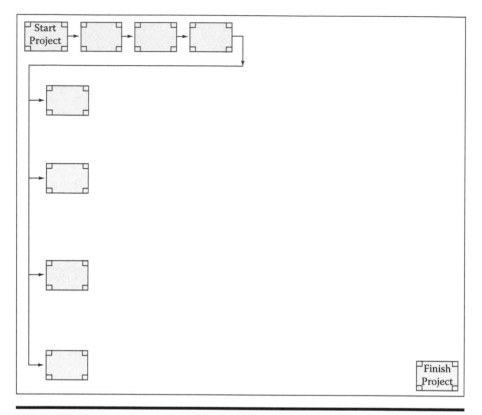

**Figure 18.19   Rearrange the network.**

We "step back" from the project-level Network and discover that something is missing. We add an extra lag of deliverables to the PBS and the corresponding extra activities (marked "E") t]o the Network (Figure 18.23).

This completes Step 5. We finish the day by identifying risks — 35 risk events are identified by brainstorming in only five minutes. We stopped and decided to pick up the effort again the next day.

## Step 6

It is the next day. We have set aside three hours to complete the Process. The project-level Network is complete and shows more than enough detail. The consensus is that we had more detail than needed. The team is experienced, and three

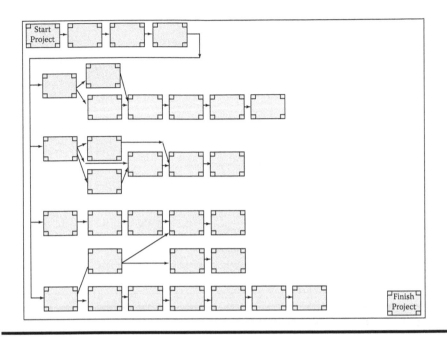

**Figure 18.20   A series of paths.**

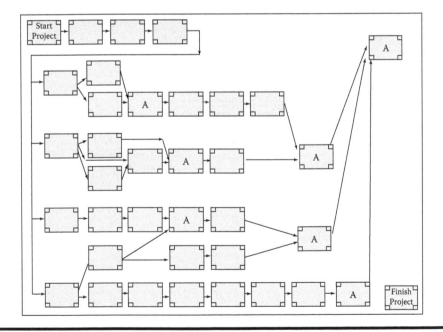

**Figure 18.21   Assembly point activities.**

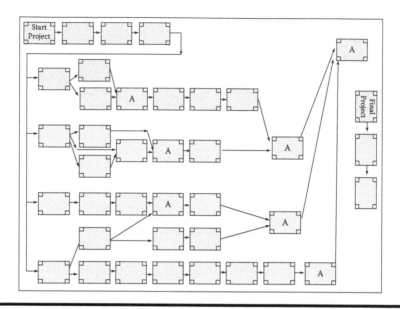

**Figure 18.22    Post-event activities.**

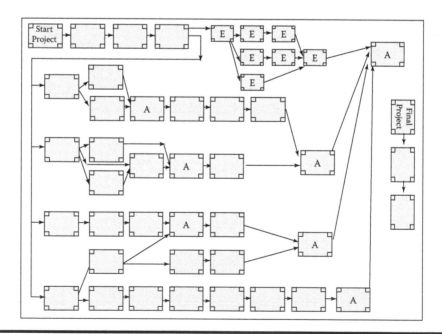

**Figure 18.23    Extra activities (marked "E").**

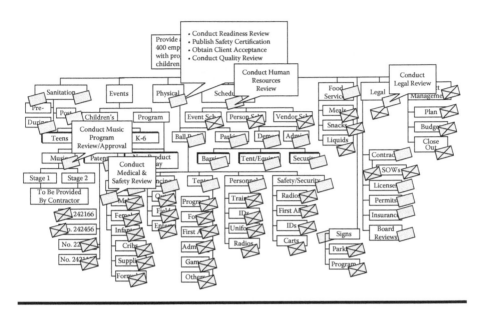

**Figure 18.24   The PBS from another point of view.**

of the four members were actively involved in the planning and execution of last year's event. This level of experience causes us to view the PBS from another point of view (Figure 18.24).

We decide that most of the lower-level deliverables (those shown here with "Xs") would remain on the PBS but not "made into" activities. Instead, these lower-level deliverables will become checklists — one list for each team member to follow and complete. The remaining deliverables make up the Network (Figure 18.25).

The team assigns either the resources' names or types (shown on the right edge). In 15 minutes, this step was complete (see Figure 18.26).

# Step 7

As soon as the resources are assigned, we start Step 7. There was no reluctance on the part of team members to provide the necessary duration estimates. There is some difficulty in estimating durations for the subcontractors' responses (deliverables) such as turn-around times for menus, specifications for fencing, tenting, electrical, and water resources — we use what we think will be average durations. The subcontractors will later validate the averages. The Post-Its are now complete with circled durations (Figure 18.26).

Our network is now ready for critical path analysis (CPA).

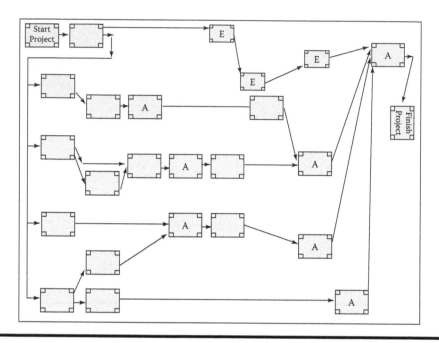

**Figure 18.25   The remaining deliverables.**

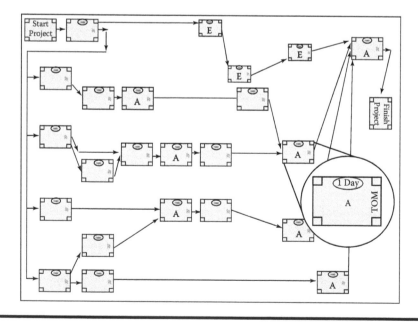

**Figure 18.26   Network is now ready for critical path analysis.**

## Step 8

Everything is ready for CPA, and the team performs CPA with very little instruction. The resulting critical path is about what we expected (see Figure 18.27).

The overall project duration is within five days of the target endpoint (on the short side). You (the reader) cannot see the detail but the critical path (now highlighted) goes through the generation and approval of subcontractors' contracts. We "work" the critical path and reduce its duration, but now we have two critical paths (Figure 18.28). The second critical path is the negotiations and contracting process with the county Board of Directors — we are using a county softball field and associated parking for the event.

## History and Lessons Learned

### *History*

You were the project manager for the facility's setup portion of this year's family recognition event. The event occurred in late spring in the southern United States. You were to provide all physical facilities as defined in this statement-of-work for the recognition event in a timely and cost-conscious manner.

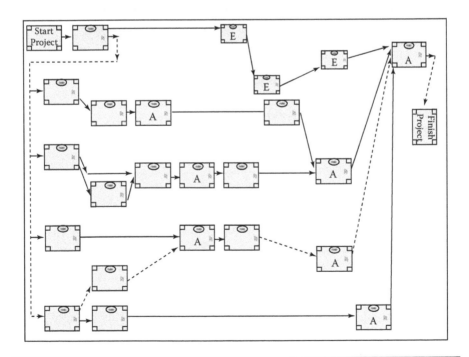

**Figure 18.27   The resulting critical path.**

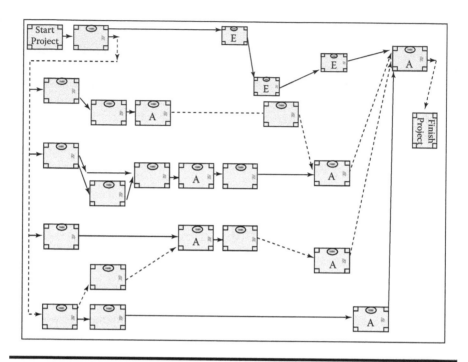

**Figure 18.28　We now have two critical paths.**

Facilities centered on these events and areas:

Live music event (7 p.m.–9 p.m.)
Demonstrations Area (1 p.m.–6 p.m.)
Children's programs (1 p.m.–6 p.m.)
Food and refreshments (1 p.m.–6 p.m.)
Safety and security (10 a.m.–10 p.m.)
Personal comfort (10 a.m.–10 p.m.)

Your setup took place between 7 a.m. Monday and 5 p.m. Thursday. The event began at 1 p.m. Friday. City inspection had to be completed and the event permit issued by 5 p.m. Thursday. You conducted a site check beginning at 6:30 p.m. Thursday.

*Site description:* The event site was the softball playing area between the Topo River and state highway 145. The site included four softball fields arranged at the corners of a "quad" with a large grassy area in the center.

Each softball field had one five-level, steel and wood set of bleachers that held approximately 100 people. These bleachers were located outside the playing fields, wrapped around the corner, and were separated from the fields by 14-feet-high spectator safety fencing.

There was parking for 145 cars located immediately to the west and south of the playing fields. Two refreshment stands were located to the north and south of the fields. These stands were the source of water and electricity. There were four open entrances to the center grassy area, one in each direction. This facility was chosen and contracted for by the event's overall planner, a professional event-planning firm.

*Your team background*: You were the site facility manager and your team consisted of Larry (an electrical contractor), Jean (a nurse and owned a day-care center), and Tom (a general building contractor and a state-licensed contractor).

*Your contractor team:* You used 100 percent contract services to provide all facilities. They were:

- "We Tent-Em" (flooring, tents, bleachers, tables, chairs)
- "AAAA Electrical" (drops, infield lighting, communications)
- "Waste General" (food and personal waste)
- "Contractors #409" (water, construction, landscaping)
- "Brooks Security" (general area and crowd barriers)
- "The Country Boys" (lighting and sound)
- "Live Play, Inc." (self-contained rides and electronic games)
- "Readi-Meals" (food and drinks)

All contractors agreed on fixed-price contracts, to be performed when the area became available and weather conditions permitted. Some night work by the contractors was necessary.

Note that an event team was in charge of the actual event, including:

- Contracting (purchasing)
- Medical (air-conditioned safety tent)
- Marketing (product displays)
- Program design (event layout)
- Security (infield security supervision)
- Communications personnel (manager and public spokesperson)
- Facilities (you)
- General Event Coordinator (professional event contractor)
- City contract

Infield areas of the ballfields were used but not significantly disrupted. Water and electrical drops were available in grassy areas only. No water was available over 150 feet from the source; no power outlets more than 200 feet from sources. Tents were floored and staked no more than 18 inches deep. Additional bleachers were available in grassy areas only. Security fencing was expandable, poly-plastic material only. Additional security entrances were possible but were manned. Spectator safety fencing at the corners of the ball diamond was removed. All efforts were made to protect the two uncovered baseball diamonds. Parking for the EMT area was clearly marked with easy access to roads and the event area. Off-road parking was not permitted. No modifications to the existing roads were allowed.

City employees were employed on the day of the event, including:

- One fire brigade (pumper truck plus crew of four)
- One EMT team (two emergency technicians plus driver)
- One fire marshal (electrical and seating safety)
- Six police officers (parking and traffic control)

City employees who were employed during the pre-event period included two groundskeepers (pre-event mowing and grounds modification approval).

*General contracting rules:*

- "We Tent-Em" did erect floored tents for the food service, food prep, and safety. They erected the live show stage, the electronic games, demonstrations, and central command areas. They erected the banquet tables for demonstration, game, and food service tents. They assembled small tables and chairs around the food service tent and provided bleachers on the grassy area between baseball diamonds A and B for 300 people. They had only two crews operating at any one time.
- "AAAA Electrical" extended the 110-Volt service to the game, food prep, food service, safety, live show, and demonstration tents. They extended 220-Volt service to the food prep tent and children's rides. They provided 300-foot-candle lighting on tripods in general areas and extended telephone service to the command tent. They handled air conditioner installation in the medical tent ONLY as their last work item. Only two crews worked at any one time. They refused to work in areas near waste or water supply workers.
- "Waste General" provided food waste collection facilities for the entire area, including toilet facilities required for 600 persons. These facilities were two self-contained "personal vans," 10 feet wide and 40 feet long and moved via normal 16-wheeled trucking rigs.
- "Contractors #409" extended water and wastewater services to the food service tent and personal vans. They provided general landscaping to the grassy area as necessary for safety. They erected crowd control barriers for food service, children's rides, games, and live show areas as necessary. They also assembled two additional bleacher sections and erected security entries of poly-plastic.
- "Brooks Security" provided entry gate security. They provided crowd control for food service and live shows.

- "The Country Boys" provided program lighting and sound.
- "Live Play, Inc." provided four to six self-contained children's rides (K–6). They provided stand-alone electronic games for up to 125 young adults.
- "Readi-Meals" provided a prep area for meals for 300 people. They provided chilled facilities for canned soft drinks for 1200 people. They provided a service area for other food items as seasonally appropriate.

## Lessons Learned

### Demography

We found that we did not have a full understanding of how many employees and their families, and their age groups (i.e., teens, middle school, K–6, babies).

Lessons learned:

1. An advanced, general announcement with a return (RSVP) letter would provide a much better understanding of quantity and types of persons expected to attend.
2. Personnel records are not a good source for decisions regarding the expected demographics.

### Safety

The unexpected numbers of people attending the event placed stress on the safety plans and the personnel involved. This was mostly evident during the exiting of the crowds at the end of the event. Our contracts for police services to cover the parking and movement in the parking areas did not cover the timeframe necessary.

Lessons learned:

1. Write the police coverage contract to extend at least one hour past the end of any planned, evening event.

### Program

The musical program was not what was expected. The band's range of music was extremely limited — 100 percent country western. The program for product demonstration was under-attended. The program for teens was underestimated with resulting crowding — commented on by those who could not utilize the equipment. The almost total lack of infants was unexpected and probably resulted from individual decisions to "leave the babies with a baby sitter."

Lessons learned:

1. Musical content should be reviewed by requiring "audition tapes" in advance of any decisions.
2. Expect 50 percent of middle-school-aged attendees to "cross over" to teen-age-level programs.

3. Special effort is necessary to make product demonstration of interest to family members.

## Food Service

The amount of food necessary was underestimated by about 25 percent, and the cause was a "fixed-price" contract with the vendor. The vendor was able to recover only because it had facilities in the immediate area and more food was eventually provided.

Lessons learned:

1. In matters concerning food, write a cost-plus contract.
2. Make special provision for alternative diets.
3. Include an inquiry as to food preferences in the RSVP letter.

## Area Controls

The control of the event ground was only just adequate. More emphasis on crowd control is required for the attendance achieved (unexpected). A ballfield may not be the best location in a southern climate with frequent rains. The use of bleachers is not appropriate for large crowds and food — tables in small groups would be better. We were surprised to see the number of individuals arriving with portable coolers (and their own beverages).

Lessons learned:

1. Find a location with a "hard" surface and one not affected by weather; consider a large indoor facility.
2. Set aside monies and areas for small groups of tables and chairs.
3. Increase the number of personnel assigned to crowd control.
4. Make it explicit that no food or beverages should be brought into the event.

# Timing

Project size assumptions include four-month duration, team of six, an intellectual project, 150 to 200 activities, and an average of two activities per week per team member.

| Step / Process | Alone | With Others |
|---|---|---|
| Step 1 | 1–2 hr | 1–2 hr (limited team) |
| Step 2 | 30–60 min | 1–2 hr (limited team) |
| Step 3 | 60–90 min(60–120 min with SME)** | 2–3 hr (limited team) |
| Step 4 | 30–60 min | Team builds PBS 2–3 hr If PBS ready, 1 to 2 hr |
| Step 5 | 1–2 hr | 1–2 hr |
| Step 6 | 10–20 min | 15–30 min |
| Step 7 | 30 min | 30–60 min |
| Step 8 | 30–60 min | 30–45 min |
| A second pass | 60 min | 1–2 hr |
| Manual scheduling | 30 min | 30–60 min |
| Scheduled network | 60 min | 30–60 min |
| Resource allocation | 60 min | 30–60 min |

# Chapter 19

## Frequently Asked Questions (FAQs)

### FAQs Related to the Session

There will be a number of questions before, during, and after the Session. This chapter discusses just a few frequently asked questions. I suggest that you prepare handouts of selected questions and distribute them. A frank, open discussion up front in the Session will clarify a number of questions your team will want answered.

**FAQ:** How will you use the plan?

Be assured that your project team will begin to speculate on how you are going to use this data. You need to get up front with your answer.

You plan to use the data to manage them and control the project. The project plan is the road map for project implementation — without a road map, you cannot possibly know where you are going. There is a danger here!. If, in fact, you will use the project plan developed by your team, then you are *good-to-go*. If, on the other hand, you decide not to use their plan but instead decide to use your own plan, therein lies the danger. It is like asking someone's opinion and then not honoring and using it. If you are the type of person who likes to set all the plans and then convince your team that yours are best, do not even consider conducting the Session. In this latter case, it is far better never to have asked their opinion.

**FAQ:** Can we modify your approach for the project?

How well your decisions regarding the direction of the project are received will depend a great deal on how you present them. You need to approach these items as you have all the other advance preparation documents — that is, as if they are only straw men. If you present them in this open, frank manner, and truly make the team feel that it can modify them, then you will achieve your results as well as a side benefit. You will get a set of decisions made by the team members and they will sense that they can really make a **difference!**

**FAQ:** What should be your project plan's architecture?

There can be different architectures for your plan. A single-string plan is a simple, uncomplicated string of activities. An example might be a project plan for an event, a wedding, a home project. This simple plan is usually sufficient for a project with few participants. A phased plan is a project plan divided into what are natural divisions — based on either time or types of effort. An example would be a project plan for a house. There is the planning and legal stage, the site preparation stage, the framing stage, etc. Hierarchical plans are multiple plans, each with its own levels and each level relating to another level through interlocking activities. Hierarchical plans lend themselves to reporting schemes implemented in different levels of management in large organizations. An example of a hierarchical project plan would be a project plan for a new product development effort with tracking by several levels of management. The plan's hierarchy provides sufficient information for each management level, yet avoids the need for management to become involved in lower-level detailed reviews. The levels of this plan are kept in synch by the interlocking common activities at the various levels.

**FAQ:** Who is the customer for the plan?

You should know by now who is the customer for the project's outcome — its product. However, who is the customer for your project plan — that is, the plan itself? Why do we need to know this answer? Depending on the answer, you might develop your project plan differently, with more or less detail. If you are entirely on your own, meaning that the project plan is for your project team's exclusive use, the amount of detail is entirely up to you and your team. However, if you have someone looking over your shoulder, a manager who expects to review progress on a regular basis, the amount of detail in your plan will vary. How it varies depends on the style of that person. If you are required to review your progress with your customer, you will probably develop a project plan with significantly less detail. However, in this case, how do you balance the need for less against the need for detail to enable you to manage using the plan? You can resolve the two distinct needs by developing a hierarchical plan with the top hierarchy used for the customer review and the lower one used with your team for managing the project.

**FAQ:** What should your policy be concerning activity granularity?

Granularity, in the way it is used here, is the smallest and largest activity — duration-wise. This subject will come up during the Session, and now it is time to make that decision. Be careful, as this decision can have a great effect on the size of your project plan. I can best explain by example. If you have a one-week project, you can set the lower granularity for one hour. That is, you will not plan any activity that takes less than one hour. In this manner, you will plan a maximum of 40 activities if you are working alone on the project. That means that you will have to plan and then track and report 40 activities. Now take an 18-month project; the same lower granularity decision would mean you could have about 3000 activities if you alone work (250 days per year times 1.5 years times 8 hours per day). That means 3000 activities to plan, track, and report, and all with only one person! In this last example, maybe a better decision would be to set your lower limit at one week. Then you have a maximum of about 75 activities. That is much better and, in addition, who really wants to hear more detail?

**FAQ:** How should individuals report their status?

There are two basic styles for reporting progress. The first is percentage complete. This style requires you to make an estimate of how much of an activity is completed as a percentage of the whole. This percentage is used to predict (calculate) when the activity can be completed. Interesting point of view: first you make an estimate of something already done. What is that, you say? Why do we need to make an estimate of something that is already done? Why not just report what is already done?

This question leads to the second technique: duration remaining. This is an improvement; we are looking at the part of the activity that we can affect. Duration remaining also is used to calculate when an activity can be completed. The problem with both of these styles is that we end up estimating some part (completed or remaining duration) of an estimate. Remember that we started with an estimate of the duration.

There is another simpler technique — binary completion. Binary completion reporting is very simple: your activity is either done (you earn "a one") or not done (you earn "a zero"). It is a simple concept; it solves the problem of reporting and can be implemented with full team acceptance. There is, of course, one problem: what if your activities are very long (say, 15 to 40 weeks)? That would mean that you would have to wait all that time, only to find out that the activity is not complete as planned. In this case, binary completion is not very different from percentage complete reporting. This problem can be partially solved by a policy — that is, "any activity on the critical path is required to be subdivided into multiple, shorter activities." In this way, I get regular reports on these now shorter activities.

**FAQ:** How often will you request progress?

Answer this question early in your project cycle and before the team finishes its planning. This question contains more than meets the eye. You might think the question implies that they are interested in the status reporting cycle. What they will not ask is: "Are you really going to use all this (i.e., project plans) to manage our project?" How you answer the original question sets the stage for your project implementation. If you waffle on this question, you could be sending a message that "This has all been fun, but now it's back to business as usual." Think hard about this decision before you even call for the planning session. I would suggest that if you are not going to use the project plan they develop, you should not ask them to develop it at all. Your "hidden" intentions will affect your team's morale. It can have the same effect as asking for their suggestions, taking them with a smile, and throwing them into the wastebasket while they are watching. You can bet they will be watching.

**FAQ:** Will you conduct formal status reviews?

Like the previous question, your answer can signal a lot to the waiting audience. Once you get past the unspoken, you will want to consider the implied question: "How often must we prepare for a status review?" Unspoken here is the implication that reporting status and the resultant discussions are not real work. If you "back off" from running regular status meetings, you will reinforce the wrong impression. You may even have to get over that same feeling for yourself. I know that when I first started out, I had the opinion that status reviews were not productive work, so I handled status information in a rather off-hand manner. My team members read me very well and soon even my off-hand gathering of status became impossible. When my manager saw what was happening, he straightened me out quickly. I will always remember those sage words: "Project planning, status reviews, etc. are real work and as much a part of the project work as coding, designing, developing, etc." Do not be timid — providing status on their activities is real work and it is their work.

**FAQ:** How often should you refresh the project plan?

This is a decision you will want to put some thought into and certainly before the planning session. By refresh, I mean a complete regeneration of the project plan from where you are now, timewise, and forward from there. It is amazing how people will plan a 12-month project and think that it will happen that way. A popular riddle asks: "When will a project plan start to become out-of-date and not reflect reality?" The answer is: "As soon as your team returns to work and starts to implement it." What you need to establish before, and announce during your planning session, is the date for your next project refresh session. I answer the question as I use one of those large European road maps. The concept is the folded map concept (Figure 19.1).

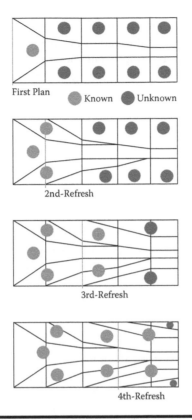

**Figure 19.1  The folded map concept.**

If I am traveling 400 kilometers in one day, I fold the map so I can see just the next 40 kilometers (First Plan). When I get about 30 kilometers into that 40, I fold the map for another 40 kilometers (2nd Refresh). At the end of the day, I have gotten where I wanted and did not fill the entire front seat (also my view) with a map. I really do not need to see any detail beyond the next 40 kilometers. This assumes, of course, that I first mapped out the complete 400 kilometers (my timeline) and generally knew how I wanted to get there. Another way of looking at this concept is your *window of knowledge.* You establish your window of knowledge so you can decide how often you need to refresh your plan. The window of knowledge is the timeframe (duration) during which you can reasonably expect to know what might happen, what you can really see clearly. It is the lapse time within a project where you can articulate project details in terms of activities, predecessors, and durations. Beyond the window of knowledge, what you can see is hazy and unclear. Your window of knowledge differs not only by project, but also by where you are currently in the project. I like to establish their window of knowledge with the complete project team sometime during the Session. I do go prepared with my own idea. I can gain further information regarding the window of knowledge by observing the amount of future detail the team members can reveal. I like to set this planning parameter by explaining my rationale and asking for their input — they set it. It is like driving a car in the fog — you do not want to "out-drive your lights."

**FAQ:** Will those attending the Session require some basic training?

That is, will those attending understand the network basis and the techniques you want them to use? You will probably find that most people will not understand the specifics of your planning technique but will rapidly grasp the concept of networks. Even among those project managers who profess to use project management, you will find that not all are "singing from the same hymnbook." If you are to perform the training, I would suggest that you provide only the minimum training necessary and just in time — that is, just before they need it.

**FAQ:** Who should attend the Session?

There is an underlying question here: "Should some people be excluded for this first session?" There is no clear answer to this question. You must consider this possibility and if the answer is "yes," then there may be other deeper questions involved. Are those assigned the right persons? Are potential personnel problems developing already? Perhaps it is a question of sheer numbers. If you have a very large team, you might want to consider developing your project plan over several sessions. Each week of plan development would result in either more detail or maybe entirely separate portions of the project (your product breakdown structure [PBS] will help you discover if there are natural divisions). Just how you organize your planning effort can depend a great deal on your team size and, to some extent, its combined team personality. Only you can sense how you need to organize this effort, but you do need to think a bit on this question

I have used another approach when my team is very large and scattered over several sites. First, we developed the PBS and it revealed the project's natural organization. Then using this natural organization, we began a series of planning sessions at the individual sites to develop their site plan. What developed was a series of plans at one level of similar detail. Then using a selected subset of the complete project team, we conducted a single planning session where we integrated these separate plans. Our next step was to combine, where possible, detailed activities into larger activities, essentially creating fewer activities with longer durations. This new hierarchy (of now fewer activities) became our project level plan. In effect, we created an integrated project-level plan ranging from very detailed plans at the individual sites to a far less detailed plan at the project control site (headquarters). This integrated project-level plan became our plan for managing the project. The site plans were intact at the sites and were used to manage and report project progress.

Control site progress reporting required a roll-up of the site progress reports for a single week, once a month. We used the integrated project plan to report overall project progress to our headquarters management team.

**FAQ:** Are there separate leaders in the Session?

I strongly recommend that you establish a list of the leaders for the Session and define their roles and authority. I distributed the list and discussed it early in the Session to clarify each role. In this way, you can avoid personal confrontations that may develop later. It really does set the stage for a smoother planning session.

**FAQ:** What should be our expectations?

First, consider the amount of activities that you can possibly plan in the time available. This really depends on the project's complexity, how clear the project's expected outcomes are, the combined and individual project personalities, etc. My experience from conducting many such sessions says that in a three-day period you can expect a project plan ranging from 200 to 250 completely planned activities.

**FAQ:** How complete should the plan be at the end of the planning session?

How many activities do you think you can get together as a plan? This is, again, a matter of how well your project team performs during the planning session. If all steps are performed, you can expect to have a plan that is roughly scheduled, has the major resource constraints resolved, and has your team's buy-in. Expect this of your session and relate your expectations to your project team early, generally within your opening address. Make a point of this and your team will get the message. Then keep them on track and extend session days as necessary to achieve it. In this manner, you will send the message that you are serious about your expectations.

**FAQ:** How are we going to handle issues?

The Process is famous for forcing out issues and you will need some techniques for handling them. First, during the session, you need a display of these issues and some process for resolving them. I take the display as one of my roles for the Process. I hear the issues, record them, and if possible, help resolve them. It is important that you control this display carefully; otherwise, this valuable aspect of the Session can get out of control and cloud your results. It is not always possible to resolve all issues during the planning session but you should try to handle as many as you can. You will want to review both the resolved and unresolved issues with the complete project team before the end of the Session. You might consider dividing issues into two categories: (1) issues and (2) concerns. Concerns are like issues but they imply less severity to the project's outcome. By the way, I call them "concerns"; you call them what you like but consider dividing them into two categories with differing severity. Finally, consider using your PC software to track them. Treat each issue and concern as an activity with predecessors, durations, and responsible person. Your PC software should have free fields you can use to code your issues and concerns as different from project activities. Defining and resolving these issues and concerns is a legitimate project planning activity.

**FAQ:** How will each activity be uniquely identified?

The Process is a simple, manual method for project plan development. What is needed is a simple means of referencing each activity. I call these references *unique identifiers* (UIs). You can make the UI a simple number or you can develop all sorts of schemes for this numbering process. I much prefer a simple whole number starting with 100. Here again, it depends on how large the project plan is and how many people are involved. Because you are reading this chapter, I will assume that you have a detailed plan. I suggest that you try my simple scheme: use ranges of values for each subset of the plan or whatever organization you have in terms of the sub-components or people. By way of an example, I assign UIs around numeric ranges by departments. Department 123 will use the 100s, department 321 will use 200s, etc.

**FAQ:** I read recently that I should be building a WBS dictionary. What is this document, and what is its value to my project?

The WBS dictionary is like a normal dictionary but for just your project; it defines your project activities — one page for each activity. I would like to recommend a WBS dictionary but I cannot do so without saying that personally I consider it the most difficult document to build. Whenever I was lucky enough to gather and distribute a WBS dictionary, it proved itself very valuable to the project team. The problem is that it is very difficult to gather and, once gathered, even more difficult to maintain up-to-date. This data is extremely valuable and will be a great source of information for you and your team. However, it is probably the least popular item you will request during the Session. Each page contains the following minimum data:

- Unique identifier (UI)
- Short activity description (the one on the Post-Its®)
- Long activity description (a 30- to 40-word paragraph)
- Completion criteria (the physical attributes of the deliverable that the project manager can use to gauge completion)
- Acceptance criteria (if this deliverable is a contracted deliverable)

In the far past, I used a paper form containing this data and requested it from the assigned person.

This really does not seem like a difficult task but you will find it one that is hard to enforce. If you can successfully obtain this data, combine it and redistribute to your team; they will also find it of value. In the recent past, I have been assembling the WBS dictionary via PCs, a wireless router, and a high-speed printer (local). This combination has worked well with information technology (IT) workers. If you plan to gather this document, I would recommend that you try some IT resources. If you are using Microsoft Project, you can include this textual data associated to the activity and in one of the user-defined text fields. Then use MS Access to report out the usual activity data and your extra information as the WBS Dictionary.

**FAQ:** How do I know if my project plan is complete?

First, I do not use the word "complete" in the same sentence with "plan." We never have a "complete plan" until the project is finished and in the lessons learned file. The question I might suggest is: "How do I know if have a sufficient plan to manage the team and control the project?"

I have studied this question from a different point of view: "Is my plan too complex?" Over a period of seven years, I kept track of more than 50 projects I helped start. What I found was that there might be a factor you can calculate at the end of the Process to help predict success for the project (plan). I call this factor the *complexity factor*.

My data showed that highly complex project plans were a predictor of project failure. You derive the complexity factor by dividing the number of predecessors (defined on each activity) by the number of activities. The smallest factor would approach one but can never reach one. The simplest network, 100 activities and 99 predecessors, will be a straight series of 100 activities and only one path. This network produces a 0.999 complexity factor. A 0.999 factor indicates that either only one person was assigned or the plan was too simple to be of any use. On the opposite end of the range, a factor of 4.8 would indicate a plan with far too much complexity. When I analyze these projects (greater than 3.5), I found there was not one project but many projects within the same project. In all these cases, the project soon failed because it could not be accomplished in the time allotted. One project was a giant SAP project for IBM, and the other was a major redirection of IBM's mid-range development community (worldwide). So what is the ideal factor for success? I would suggest a complexity factor range of between 1.9 and 2.8. The majority of the projects I followed seem to be in that range. What do you do if at the end of the Process you find that your resultant plan is outside that range? I do not have a set answer and there probably should not be one. That condition has to cause some analysis and thought on your part — that is why you are paid all that extra money.

# FAQs Regarding Post Session

**FAQ:** How are you going to handle changes to scope?

Scope is the content of the project, the deliverables — the expectations of your customer. Your preparation for the Session plus the project plan itself will establish your project's scope. The question is: How do you handle changes coming from your customer, your management, yourself, and your team? You will need to set up, in advance of the project implementation, a process that shows how you will handle scope change requests. The change process need not be a complicated procedure but you do need to put some sense of formality. Do not just let it happen! A little thought ahead of time and a full discussion during your planning session will go a long way toward eliminating these problems with their inherent confusion and misunderstandings.

**FAQ:** Will you use PC software?

This decision should be established well in advance of your planning session. If you chose not to use software to support your project, then you will approach the size of your project plan differently than if you chose to use software. Then there is the problem of what software to use. The selection of project management software is not a trivial matter. It can be a question of cost but more often, you need to make it a question of its ease of data input, its processing functions, and its ease of output. These selections can be time consuming, and the final results can greatly affect your productivity as the project manager. If you decide not to use PC software, then how will you maintain your plan? You need to consider this possibility. You need not always use computers to maintain your project plans. The chapter on "manual tracking and reporting" will give you an alternative.

**FAQ:** What is the best PC software to maintain resources once I get them?

I thought on this for a while and realized that, as far as I know, there is no software for this specific purpose. However, I have a few ideas for obtaining and maintaining personal commitments from your team members throughout the entire project. There is no substitute for gaining commitment to the Process. There is no substitute for a team-based planning process of **any kind.** Any method you use that brings together your team and facilitates a team plan is good. There is no substitute for a face-to-face commitment, sealed by a handshake. Once obtained, commitments maintenance is really a matter of the project manager's style and the environment the project "lives in." These processes put the project manager in the best position to see that personal commitments are maintained. Maintaining a commitment starts before an activity is executed — checking with each team member periodically, but certainly just before his or her activity is scheduled to begin. I use my PC software to generate special reports: sorted by critical path, early start, and assigned person, and then paged on assigned person. These reports help me keep track of my team's commitments and help me review their individual workloads and resources. In this manner, I am keeping their commitments "in front" of the individuals and helping them anticipate any changes. Resource commitments are like a currency — you spend it wisely.

Even during and after completion (of an activity), you stay in touch with the assigned person and help when you can to manage their workload. After their activity is completed, your team members need to know how you think they performed — what were their strong points and where they might improve. This final action provides the human need for closure and is a solid demonstration of your humanity and project management style.

**FAQ:** I am planning to use Microsoft Project as my PC software. How do I "translate" your Post-It format into Microsoft Project?

A completed Post-It (after Step 7) has all the information you require to enter the plan into MS Project. The difficulty is the predecessors. The Process develops the predecessors as unique identifiers. Project does not automatically recognize unique identifiers. You have to express the relationships (predecessors) in the form that Project uses — sequence numbers. The sequence numbers are contained in the first column of data (Gantt view), and you have no control over them. As you enter an activity, it is assigned a sequence number — next in the series. The problem is that MS Project uses these sequence numbers exclusively to define the predecessors.

Your first step is to define two new text fields in Project: UI and Relation (Figure 19.2). Once defined, you can now enter the activities data: UI, Description, Duration, Responsible, and Relation (Figure 19.3).

Once you have entered your data, you can establish the activity's predecessor. Establishing the predecessor is simple but a little confusing. Start by finding the sequence number that matches an activity's predecessor. In this example, you are looking for the sequence number that matches the relation 211 for activity 204. Sequence number 4 matches unique identifier 211 and the 4 is entered in activity

**Gantt View of MS Project**

Note: Insert the columns in Red

| Seq No | IU | Description | Duration | Responsible | Relation | Predecessors |
|--------|----|-------------|----------|-------------|----------|--------------|
|  |  |  |  |  |  |  |

**Figure 19.2   Add two columns to Gantt view of MS Project.**

**Gantt View of MS Project**

| Seq No | IU | Description | Duration | Responsible | Relation | Predecessors |
|--------|-----|-------------|----------|-------------|----------|--------------|
| 1 | 204 | deeeddee | 2 | Tom | 211 | |
| 2 | 144 | eeeeeeee | 12 | Larry | 204,199 | |
| 3 | 199 | rrrrrrrr | 5 | Writer | 119 | |
| 4 | 211 | dddddddd | 2 | Pmer | 231 | |
| 5 | 119 | dffffffff | 3 | MGR | 265 | |

**Figure 19.3    Enter the activities data.**

204's Relation column (Figure 19.4). In this manner, the remaining predecessors are found and entered (Figure 19.5). This process can be confusing but it can be accomplished quickly with a team of at least two persons. By the way, as you enter additional activities, the sequence numbers are automatically entered for you. If you insert an activity between activities already entered, the sequence numbers that follow will automatically increase by 1. Do not worry, as MS Project also automatically changes the predecessor for you.

# FAQs Regarding Project Management in General

**FAQ:** Recently, I attended a lecture on project management and the speaker kept referring to "your style." What is the project manager's style, and why is it important?

The word "style" seems to have two possible meanings with regard to a project manager. The first meaning might be: a particular type or sort, with reference to form, appearance, or character. I like to think of style as his or her personal approach to almost everything regarding projects. A second meaning might be the documents that must accompany every project. This second style is like a "style document" in writing — a document that defines the paragraphs, the spacing, the heading, the fonts, etc. It's "the rules of the road" for writing a document. Your project documents will reveal your style for handling the many situations you will meet in

**Gantt View of MS Project**

| Seq No | IU | Description | Duration | Responsible | Relation | Predecessors |
|--------|-----|-------------|----------|-------------|----------|--------------|
| 1 | 204 | deeeddee | 2 | Tom | 211 | 4 |
| 2 | 144 | eeeeeeee | 12 | Larry | 204,199 | ↑ |
| 3 | 199 | rrrrrrrr | 5 | Writer | 119 | |
| 4 | 211 | dddddddd | 2 | Pmer | 231 | |
| 5 | 119 | dffffffff | 3 | MGR | 265 | |

**Figure 19.4   Sequence number 4 matches unique identifier 211.**

**Gantt View of MS Project**

| Seq No | IU | Description | Duration | Responsible | Relation | Predecessors |
|--------|-----|-------------|----------|-------------|----------|--------------|
| 1 | 204 | deeeddee | 2 | Tom | 211 | 4 |
| 2 | 144 | eeeeeeee | 12 | Larry | 204,199 | 1,3 |
| 3 | 199 | rrrrrrrr | 5 | Writer | 119 | 5 |
| 4 | 211 | dddddddd | 2 | Pmer | 231 | ↑ |
| 5 | 119 | dffffffff | 3 | MGR | 265 | |

**Figure 19.5   Remaining predecessors are found and entered.**

projects. You need to concern yourself with this fact and knowing that others will be looking for your style — so perfect your writing skills.

I am not sure which of these styles your speaker was referring to but it gives me this opportunity to talk about your "project manager style." Your style is not something you are born with, like your physical appearance, but rather it is something you learn as you experience project after project. Your observation of other project managers (hopefully successful ones) is a method of developing your style quickly. Observe their style, select from their style those styles that will work for you, and adopt them. There is a comment you will frequently hear in project management sessions: lacking any authority, a little style goes a long way.

**FAQ:** I have read about a "charter." Just what is it, and what is its value to me?

Project management (literature) uses the term "charter" in many contexts. The charter I am familiar with is a document defining the project manager's authority and accountability. The charter most often "speaks" only of authority and responsibility. I much prefer my version — *authority* without defined *accountability* is only one half of a proper delegation.

Generally, the project manager writes the project charter for the project's sponsor (client?). The question of who can delegate authority is a "sticking point." In simplest terms, the sponsor is the person who has the money, reviews progress, decides on requested changes, and ultimately decides whether the project was a success. The sponsor's actions are important because he is, in fact, extracting items of accountability from the project manager.

The basic authority items are to (1) manage the project, (2) expend resources, and (3) be the single point of communication regarding the project. The corresponding accountability (points) are to (1) plan, execute, and report progress on a periodic basis, (2) report planned-to-actual expenditures on a periodic basis, and (3) maintain an open communications log for review on a periodic basis.

A charter is ideally no longer that one page on both sides. The charter is of value to the project manager to declare to all interested persons, his or her authority and limits. Past project problems can be either reduced or eliminated by a properly written authority item. I wish I could give you a reference to the matter of *charter* but as of this writing, I have found none that I would value.

**FAQ:** My project team is scattered across the United States and in Europe. How can a project plan be developed under these conditions?

Your project situation is being duplicated many times each day — a very common situation in our worldwide economies. There is no simple answer at this time. Very little is written about a *virtual project team*, which is the new name for this situation. I have had only limited experience in this environment. My single project that was truly a virtual project (team) was a major effort by IBM to reorganize their mid-range computer development labs. In that case, I had to "travel" the plan. Each week for nine months, I traveled to the different sites and, while there, helped them develop their portion of the overall plan. After gathering the separate site's plans, I combined them (with the help of a number of very capable people). It took nine months and the project was to be complete in 28 months. Finally, those in charge reviewed the project plan and asked only one question: "Is this project doable?" It did not take long to gather consensus: "No, not in this timeframe and in the current development environment."

Another method is to "travel" your team to a central location for a set period. This is difficult because of costs but the "real" difficulty is because management does not understand. They do not understand the value of working face-to-face with your team, and them with each other. They do not understand why you (the project manager) cannot just develop the plan yourself. They just do not understand, period.

This leaves it to you to develop the plan yourself. Then how do you gain and keep the team members' commitment?

I hope that soon some project manager does develop a better method for gathering the project plan from a virtual team. His or her task cannot be considered complete until they write and disseminate their method — write a book, write an article, make a presentation. Sorry, no simple answers here.

# Chapter 20

## Essay
## *The WBS — Worth a Second Look*

[*Author Note:* This essay was presented at several PMI regional meetings in 2002 and 2003. Recent research has clarified my knowledge of the origin of the WBS (work breakdown structure), and this new information is included in the body of this book. This essay is reproduced here as it was presented then.]

The work breakdown structure (WBS) is considered by many project managers as a tool for developing their project plan — most view it as only a means to that end. In fact, it is my opinion that most project managers wrongly view it as only the Gantt display in their project software. On the other hand, I view the WBS as both an essential step to a project plan and an end unto itself (Figure 20.1, Figure 20.2).

My presentation will cover:

1. The WBS and its origin,
2. How our understanding of the WBS has evolved
3. How to best build and use it during the execution of projects (Figure 20.3)

### The WBS and Its Origin

The WBS and its origin — the exact date when the WBS was developed and the reason for development — has disappeared from my body of knowledge of project

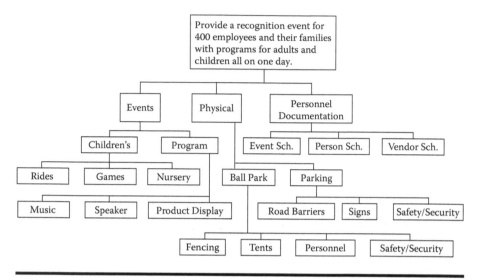

**Figure 20.1    Topmost level deliverable.**

```
1.0 Provide a recognition ...
    1.1 Events
        1.1 Children's
        1.1.2 Program
    1.2 Physical
    1.3 Personal Documentation
        1.3.1 Event Sch.
        1.3.2 Person Sch.
        1.3.3 Vendor Sch.
```

**Figure 20.2    The outline format.**

- The Work Breakdown Structure (WBS) and its origin.
- How our understanding of the WBS has evolved.
- How to best build and use it.

**Figure 20.3    Organization of the presentation.**

**Figure 20.4   Project management folklore in the making.**

management. By far, the majority of my knowledge concerning the WBS seems to be based on project management folklore (Figure 20.4).

The first reference to the WBS I became aware of was an article in a magazine in 1988 — and I have since lost even that article. I seem to remember a diagram showing the relationships between a deliverable, an activity, and an organization (Figure 20.5). That article established that the WBS consists of three components:

1. The product breakdown structure (PBS),
2. The activity breakdown structure (ABS)
3. The organizational breakdown structure (OBS)

It made clear the relationship between deliverables and activities, but the organization relationship was not at all clear. The unanswered question was: "Is the

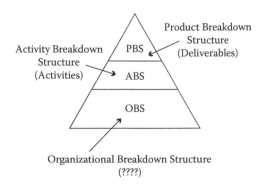

**Figure 20.5   Earliest version of the WBS.**

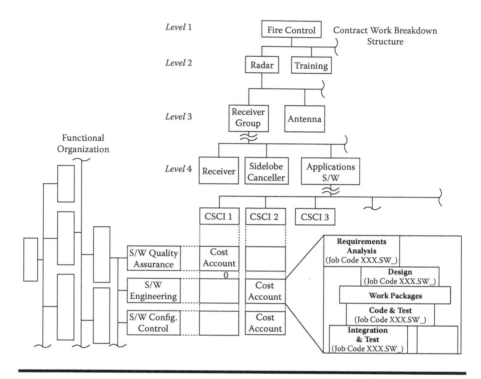

**Figure 20.6   Organization-to-deliverable relationship.**

organization breakdown structure the deliverables-to-activity relationship or is it the organization (enterprise) that was either producing the deliverables or performing the activities?" The diagrams of the organization breakdown structure concept, as I remember it, showed a matrix-like relationship between deliverables and organizational entities (departments) (Figure 20.6).

I remember being puzzled at the time by this diagram and its implied orientation but I did not see a need to pursue. While searching for a reference of the WBS for my first book (1993), I became aware of the value of the World Wide Web (WWW) as a research tool. I found a Web site that described the WBS and why it was developed. The materials on the Web site were dated 1987. That Web site disappeared sometime in 2001. The WBS diagrams were all related to Department of Defense (DoD) projects. It established the purpose of the WBS as a tool for managing a project — actually, as I remember, it really never mentioned the concept of "managing a project." I just sensed that managing a project was the purpose. In addition, the reference really never established the orientation of the WBS. By orientation, I mean whether a WBS is activity based or whether it is deliverable based — more on this point later.

The reference did not solve the mystery of why the WBS was developed for the DoD in the first place. I know that before 1988 the DoD was having difficulty completing projects on time and within budget. I can only guess that the budgetary problem prompted the development of the WBS. If so, then a piece of project management folklore comes into play.

In the early 1990s, I was involved in project management training and consulting. At that time, I engaged a number of senior project managers whose lifetime experiences as consultants included the development of many of our current project management tools. During that time, we spent many hours discussing project management concepts and tools. An outstanding example of that folklore was *the inside information regarding the development of PERT and the WBS.* These gentlemen had been involved as consultants to the DoD, the U.S. Air Force, and the U.S. Navy in the Polaris submarine program in the mid-1950s. They were part of a larger team that developed the concept of, the algorithms for, and the first diagrams of PERT.

However, because the Polaris program was top-secret, their PERT concept was taken back to California, filed, and never published. In the early 1970s, the DoD and the General Accounting Office (GAO) of the U.S. Government engaged the same consulting group. This time, they were instrumental in the development of the WBS. Be assured that this bit of folklore is based on their professional word and credibility, and my powers of recall. Because they were working with the GAO, I have made the extrapolation as to "why the WBS was developed."

What was the problem? I am willing to bet that the problem the GAO was trying to solve was: What are we paying for? One of the major roles of the GAO is to pay the government's bills. In that capacity and as good accountants, the GAO would want to understand the relationship between an invoice from a contractor and the value that the U.S. Government would receive (a deliverable). Their knowing this relationship would be absolutely necessary in order for the GAO to fulfill its mandate. My extrapolation — if you will allow me an extrapolation from what is essentially folklore — then would be that the organization breakdown structure can be essentially a numbering scheme that shows the relationship between value received (a deliverable) and an invoiced expense. The OBS is the numbering scheme you can use to relate deliverables, sub-deliverables, components, parts, and pieces in their hierarchy. An accountant would call this scheme a chart of accounts (Figure 20.7).

This numbering scheme, to an accountant, provides a traceable relationship between moneys they will pay out and the deliverable components of the project.

*Older supporting source:* My extrapolation is supported by the oldest project management book in my library — *Managing High-Technology Programs and Projects,* by Russell D. Archibald (1976, ISBN 0-471-03308-1, page 147). Archibald calls this numbering scheme "... a cost coding scheme (chart of account)."

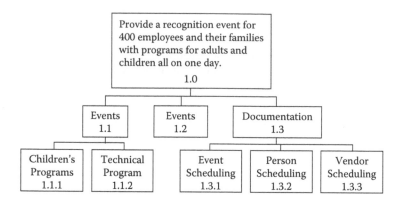

**Figure 20.7    WBS with its OBS.**

*Recent supporting sources:* There are several recent, public sources that also support my extrapolation:

1. *The DoD Web site.* The current DoD Web site does support, in part, my extrapolation. It describes the WBS in general terms but seems to emphasize the costing and cost accounting aspects of the WBS. The www URL for this site is www.acq.osd.mil/pm/newpolicy/WBS/mil_hdbk_881/mil_hdbk. html. The materials on this site are all dated: 2jan1998.

2. *PMI Practice Standard.* the second reference is the PMI Practice Standard for WBS. This reference uses a numbering scheme in all its example diagrams; they call it a coding scheme. There are some references to costs and cost accounting but no direct reference is made to the coding scheme as an accounting tool. This document can be obtained from the PMI Web site at www.pmi.org. This document was developed by a committee of PMI members and first became available in 2001. I will be using this document later to make another point.

## Our Understanding of How the WBS Has Evolved

I believe that over a period as long as 25 years, the project management profession has developed a generally accepted definition of the WBS. I am concerned that the accepted definition is not conducive to its successful, practical application in a real project environment. My use of the WBS during a project and its resultant value to the project have evolved significantly and very positively. The value and use, as originally posed in my early project management training, was slight — if at all. There was little reference to the WBS and certainly no description of how to develop it. As a new project manager, I had little idea of its value to my projects.

**Figure 20.8  The search.**

My search for truth in this glaring difference between what I was taught and the experience I developed, caused me to search for the truth — what is the true meaning of a WBS? This became my search for the "holy grail" of project management. It became an intelligential point-of-honor (Figure 20.8).

## The Search

My hypothesis is this: our understanding of the WBS appears to be very much a product of project management folklore and therefore my interpretation is just as valid as the next.

## Sources of Our Understanding

Lacking any credible source for its history, I began my search for any bits of folklore that would ultimately make up our understanding of the WBS. There are, of course, many publications containing different authors' views of the WBS. On this subject, I have read over 25 recent books and over 60 older books (prior to 1994) on this subject. I found an almost singular view of the WBS — one consistent with U.S.

Government publications of the 1980s. What I found interesting was an almost total lack of instructions on how to develop a WBS. If these authors approached the subject at all, they either reiterated the DoD point of view or they described "how important it was to develop your WBS." Gee, that was obvious to me already!

I then considered another source — commercial personal computer software for project management. My review of these sources provided, again, a consistent view of the WBS — albeit different than the one I developed by experience. This view was at least more practical in nature than that provided by the project management publications. Because of the wide distribution of this software, I now consider these sources as probably the true sources of our folklore concerning the WBS.

*The software sources:* The first software source and the most easily accessible were the operating instructions for the earlier releases (4.0) of Microsoft Project. Unfortunately, I now have only the 1998 version and it makes no reference to the WBS. Microsoft has repeatedly promised to bring its description of a WBS in line with the new, accepted definition of a WBS. But I will bet that Microsoft will tie the WBS to the Gantt chart — making it appear that a WBS is the Gantt chart (Figure 20.9).

This Microsoft Project tie-in — between the WBS (field) and the Gantt chart — has, in my opinion, caused a misinterpretation of the WBS.

Support for my assertion lies in a 1995 book by J. Davidson Frame and supports my assertion. In his book [*Managing Projects in Organizations*], Dr. Frame states on page 171 that "a true work-breakdown structure is product focused." He goes on to

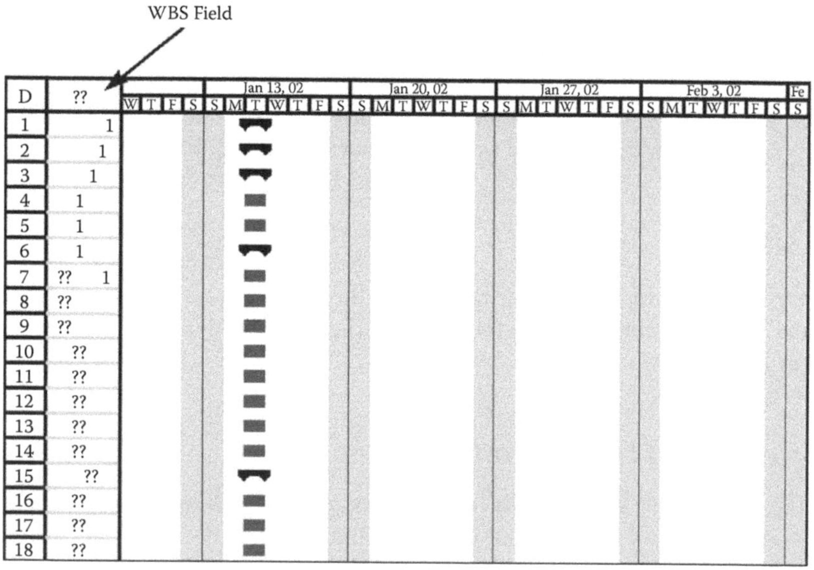

WBS Field

| D | ?? | Jan 13, 02 | Jan 20, 02 | Jan 27, 02 | Feb 3, 02 | Fe |
|---|----|------------|------------|------------|-----------|-----|
| 1 | 1 | | | | | |
| 2 | 1 | | | | | |
| 3 | 1 | | | | | |
| 4 | 1 | | | | | |
| 5 | 1 | | | | | |
| 6 | 1 | | | | | |
| 7 | ?? 1 | | | | | |
| 8 | ?? | | | | | |
| 9 | ?? | | | | | |
| 10 | ?? | | | | | |
| 11 | ?? | | | | | |
| 12 | ?? | | | | | |
| 13 | ?? | | | | | |
| 14 | ?? | | | | | |
| 15 | ?? | | | | | |
| 16 | ?? | | | | | |
| 17 | ?? | | | | | |
| 18 | ?? | | | | | |

**Figure 20.9  Microsoft Project Gantt view.**

say: "... however, today's scheduling convention — as reflected in scheduling software — leads to task lists being called work-breakdown structures. In this book, I stick with the existing convention." So as I see it, my extrapolation from folklore is actually supported by one of our profession's most prolific authors.

The second software source, and one not readily available, is the operating instructions for ABT's Workbench. I have traced this document to sometime in the early 1980s and to Workbench's developers in Great Britain. Their description is quite lengthy and probably the original source of the WBS misinterpretation. If I compare the Workbench document and the Microsoft document, I could easily make a case that Microsoft used materials from the Workbench document. So, based on this guess, I am certain that ABT is our ultimate source of how we view today the concept of a WBS.

The misinterpretations ... as I said before, my training on the WBS was significantly different from my experience. As a consultant and project manager, I have started well over 60 projects and as my experience base grew, I found the WBS to be more and more a valuable part of the planning process. I have made the statement many times: "If we cannot define the WBS, then we will not be successful." I supported this position many times by refusing to proceed until the WBS was as complete as physically possible. In all this time, many experienced project managers have challenged three of my assertions:

1. The WBS is not Microsoft's Gantt display.
2. The WBS is product (deliverable) oriented.
3. All work (work package, tasks, effort) is not at the bottom of the WBS (Figure 20.10).

Let us look at each misinterpretation to maybe understand its source and my assertion.

*Misinterpretation 1:* The first misinterpretation is this: the WBS is the Gantt display in Microsoft Project. Three years ago, I began teaching a course on managing information technology Projects; and probably in over 95 percent of the occasions, my class would point to Microsoft Project's Gantt view as the WBS. I now believe that Dr. Frame has cleared this misinterpretation by calling it "a convention." I can accept this convention like I can accept that most management call a

---

• The (WBS) is not Microsoft's Gantt display.
• The WBS is product (deliverable) oriented.
• All work (work packages, tasks, effort) is not at the bottom of the WBS.

**Figure 20.10  My assertions.**

precedence diagram a PERT chart and most people call an adjustable wrench a crescent wrench or a tissue a Kleenex. I would appeal to you, at least for yourself, to make a distinction. The distinction is the difference between a WBS and a schedule. The WBS is the basis for the schedule, not the schedule itself and certainly not Microsoft Project's view.

*Misinterpretation 2:* The second misinterpretation is this: the WBS is activity oriented. I have argued against this point for many years but I am encouraged by recent events. As I said earlier, three years ago, I began teaching a project management course. During each class, I also asked my students: "Is the orientation of the WBS by deliverable or by activity?" The first year, the majority reply was: "Activity oriented." Now, just into the fourth year, the majority reply is: "Deliverable oriented." This shift in the view of the WBS orientation has probably been driven by recent publications and a PMI study.

The DoD Web site states that the WBS is product oriented. The PMI practice guide for WBS states that the WBS is deliverable oriented — then all of its diagrams are activity oriented? A 2001 study by PMI volunteers concluded that the WBS is deliverable oriented but, "… that it could contain activities." Although the view is changing within the ranks of practicing project managers, those contributing to our body of knowledge still show the WBS as activity oriented. I would have to question whether those who are writing about project management have ever built a WBS.

*Misinterpretation 3:* The third misinterpretation is this: all work packages are at the bottom levels of the WBS. I have been fighting this statement for years and I had pretty well given up hope of changing the profession's view until recently. This misinterpretation has, in part, been changed by the profession's growing acceptance that the WBS is deliverable oriented. If in fact the WBS is deliverable oriented, I have to ask: "How can the bottom levels of the WBS contain all the work (activities)?" The new convention of "deliverable orientation" flies in face of the persistent written statement that "all work is at the bottom level." As my experience with the WBS grew, so did my realization that the WBS is started best as a deliverable-oriented diagram. I soon realized that a pure deliverable orientation would not solve all my practical problems in guiding a project team through developing their plan. The problem was that the contracted deliverables did not fully describe all the work to be performed. At that time, I added another step to my WBS build process. This step took into account those intermediate deliverables that are necessary for the team but not delivered to the client — deliverables such as specifications, strategies, designs, etc. Also, I soon realized that a pure reliance on the deliverables as a basis for the activities would cause the team to miss a considerable number of activities related to the combining of low-level deliverables into higher-level deliverables. These activities are the integration, testing, and customer relationship activities of any project. I call them the "the glue activities." They bring together all the sub-deliverables into a final deliverable. So, maybe now you can understand, if only through my thought process, how the definition of the WBS may have evolved.

## *How to Best Build and Use the WBS*

I started using the WBS in my projects with mixed results. However, over time and with lots of experience, I developed a project planning process based on the WBS (Figure 20.11).

In my recent book (to be released today [2002]), I call it the Visual Project Planning & Scheduling (VPP&S) process. Let me share with you an outline of this process. The VPP&S process is a fairly intuitive process that has been developed over many years and many projects. It is a process that lends itself to modification as the situation calls (Figure 20.12).

Step 1: In building the initial PBS during Step 1, you will begin to organize your project's scope — its deliverables. You will begin by developing the initial product breakdown structure with Post-Its®. You end with a presentation of your PBS to your client (Figure 20.13).

Step 2: In building down the PBS during Step 2, you will build down your initial product breakdown structure by adding additional deliverables — Post-Its. You will complete your preparation for the project planning session.

Step 3: In establishing the activities during Step 3, you will engage your project team at the start of the project planning session by showing and discussing the initial PBS. You then will lead them through a buy-in process

**Figure 20.11 My project planning process: my recent book cover.**

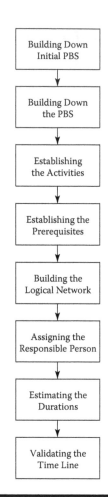

**Figure 20.12    A flowchart of the VPP&S process.**

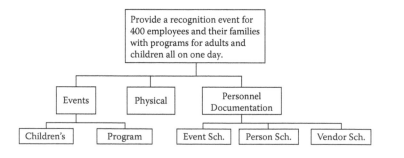

**Figure 20.13    Presentation of your PBS to your client.**

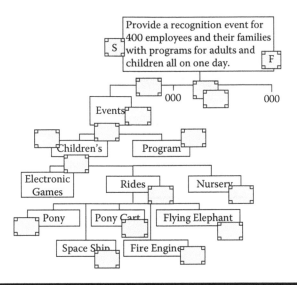

**Figure 20.14   Post-Its overlaying the PBS.**

of modifying the PBS and developing their activities. The result is their activity breakdown structure built from Post-Its and overlaying the PBS (Figure 20.14).

Step 4: In establishing the prerequisites during Step 4, your team members will develop their activity's relationships — their prerequisites. They will refine their activities' Post-Its (Figure 20.15).

Step 5: In building the logical network during Step 5, your team will construct their logical network from their ABS. They will continue to refine both their ABS and their PBS (Figure 20.16).

Step 6: In assigning the responsible person during Step 6, your team will assign the responsible persons to each activity's Post-Its. They will continue to refine their PBS and ABS (Figure 20.17).

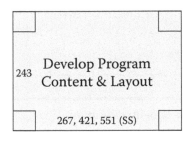

**Figure 20.15   Their prerequisites.**

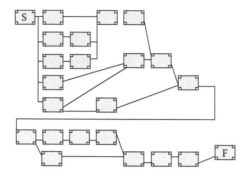

**Figure 20.16    Building the logical network.**

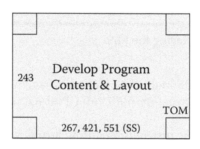

**Figure 20.17    Assign the responsible persons.**

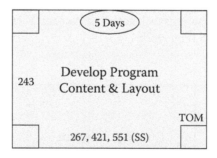

**Figure 20.18    Estimate the activity's duration.**

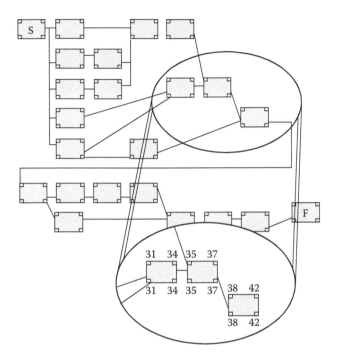

**Figure 20.19   Calculate the critical path.**

Step 7: In estimating the durations during Step 7, your team will develop their estimates of their activity's duration and add it to their Post-Its. They will continue to refine their PBS and ABS (Figure 20.18).

Step 8: In validating the timeline during Step 8, your team will perform critical path analysis to establish their project's critical path (paths). They will continue to refine their PBS and ABS and recalculate the critical path (paths) (Figure 20.19).

In conclusion, I would like to thank you, the Rochester, New York, chapter of the PMI for inviting me to your meeting today.

# Index